Essential Maths

5

Jayashri Bhattacharya

Preface

Mathematics has always been an integral part of human life. From times immemorial, Mathematics has been in our everyday life in various ways irrespective of our knowledge of the mathematical concepts involved in various activities. The school curriculum focuses on the mathematical concepts to cultivate thinking and developing the reasoning skills. It enables the students to take up a systematic approach to solve their daily life problems, aims at exploring multiple aspects of the subject and thus develop a passion for it.

Essential Maths is a series that strives to focus on the maximum involvement of children following an interactive learning pattern. It has been authored by a senior teacher who has been dedicating her years to the teaching of this subject. Following this series will help students to keep away from rote learning and develop their confidence. Their increased confidence and flexibility with numbers will help them handle abstractions and develop logical approach towards the subject. The review exercises help the learners assess their understanding of the concepts. This series also develops the potential of the learners for continuous and comprehensive evaluation, by inculcating the scholastics and co-scholastic skills. Its activity based interactive style will sharpen the learners' minds and make learning enriching and joyous. The books are beautifully illustrated which adds to the overall appeal of the series.

From the Author

Mathematics has always been an integral part of human life. We use mathematics in our everyday life in various ways without being aware of our knowledge of the mathematical concepts involved in the activity. School curriculum includes the study of Mathematics in order to focus on mathematical concepts which help to cultivate the thinking and reasoning skills. It is a systematic approach to enable students to solve their daily life problems. It also aims to allow the students to explore the multiple aspects of the subject and develop a passion for it.

The lab activities and exercises can be used by the teachers as a demonstrative tool in the Maths Lab.

Objectives of teaching Mathematics are:

- To develop an ability to think and reason mathematically
- To handle abstractions
- To cultivate a positive attitude towards mathematics following an interactive learning pattern to help the teacher ensure maximum involvement of the learners
- To increase confidence and flexibility of the learners when numbers are concerned
- To discourage rote learning
- To develop logical sense along with a passion for the subject

The series **Essential Maths** is a carefully graded series prepared in accordance with the new syllabus prescribed by the NCERT on the basis of CCE (Continuous and Comprehensive Evaluation). A remarkable feature of this series is that all the exercises are formed in such a manner that they begin with easy exercises and gradually progresses to difficult ones. The books are activity based and extensive drilling with integrated revision exercises form its key feature. All the books are full of colourful illustrations which make learning a joy! They also inculcate scholastic and co-scholastic skills in the learner.

I take this opportunity to thank a few people who have helped me write this series. They are Ms Seema Chawla my editor for continuously guiding me, my friend Ms Tapasi (Managing Editor, B Jain), my parents-in-law for encouraging me and Aurobindo, my husband, for being very supportive. Heartfelt thanks to Sofia and Shantanu, my kids. Without their suggestions and criticism, I would not have been able to undertake and complete this project.

Jayashri Bhattacharya

Contents

1 Revision

1. Write the number names for the following.

   a. 34,117

   b. 2,17,148

   c. 575,439

   d. 600,306

   e. 19,00,030

   f. 850,013

2. Write the numeral for the following number names.

   a. Twenty thousand and four

   b. Fifty thousand sixteen

   c. Nine lakh ten

   d. Six lakh five thousand sixty

   e. Seventy thousand seventy

3. Answer the following.

   a. How many thousands make a lakh?

   b. How many hundreds make a lakh?

   c. How many tens make a ten thousand?

4. Find the difference in the place values of 8 in 84,879.

5. a. Write the smallest number using the digits 6, 9, 3, 1 and 0 (only once)

   b. Write the greatest number using the digits 2, 4, 0, 5 , 8 and 7 (only once)

6. Add

   The greatest 6-digit number and the smallest 5-digit number

7. Subtract

   The sum of two numbers is 104001. If one number is 56878, the other number is ____________

8. The difference between two numbers is 178623. If the larger number is 352410, find the smaller number.

9. Fill in the blanks

   a. 26432 × 10 =

   b. 764 × 1000 =

   c. 425 × 600 =

   d. 97 × 700 =

   e. 515 × 8000 =

10. Find the product

   a. 3421 × 123

   b. 5565 × 315

   c. 9582 × 500

   d. 3751 × 121

   e. 2907 × 477

11. Divide

a. 7382136 ÷ 523

b. 87212 ÷ 123

c. 315875 ÷ 441

d. 12440 ÷ 120

e. Greatest number of 6 digits ÷ greatest number of 3 digits

12. Simplify

a. $108 \div (72 \div 6) \times 5 + 3 =$ ______________

b. $40 - \{(14 - 3) \div (20 - 9)\} + 20 =$ ______________

2 Large Numbers

The place value chart for the first 7 places in our number system is given below.

Indian Place Value System

Periods	Lakhs		Thousands		Ones		
Largest 7- digit	TL	L	TTh	Th	H	T	O
Number	9	9	9	9	9	9	9

It is ninety-nine lakh ninety nine thousand nine hundred ninety nine.

Successor of 99,99,999 is 99,99,999 + 1 = 1,00,00,000

We read 1,00,00,000 as 1 crore.

It is the smallest 8- digit number. Extending the place value chart we introduce the crores period.

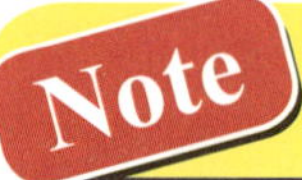

The digits in the same period are read together.

	Crores		Lakhs		Thousands		Ones		
	TC	C	TL 10,00,000	L 1,00,000	Ten Th 10,000	Thousands 1000	Hundred 100	Tens 10	Ones 1
1.	5	8	3	9	4	7	2	1	6
2.	3	7	1	8	0	5	1	2	4
3.		6	0	0	3	0	9	7	1

The first number is fifty eight crore, thirty nine lakhs, forty seven thousands, two hundred and sixteen.

In a place value chart, every time a number is increased 10 times, it shifts to a place to its left. If 30 lakhs is increased ten times the digit 3 shifts one place to its left. A new place is created-in this case, called 'crore'.

Exercise 2.1

1. Write the number name for

a.	586475	f.	9000017
b.	2316001	g.	7650489
c.	56001010	h.	4000004

2. Mark the periods and then read the numbers. (Population of states in USA)

Michigan	10003422
Ohio	11485910
Texas	24326974
California	36756666
Georgia	9685744

3. Write the place value of the underlined digits.

    a. $65\underline{3}672491$

    b. $4\underline{3}1326008$

    c. $56\underline{2}319300$

    d. $5019\underline{4}8346$

    e. $98\underline{8}93048$

    f. $\underline{6}3488800$

4. Write the numerals for

   a. Three crore, twenty lakh one

   b. Sixty nine crore, seventy thousand nineteen

   c. Fifty crore five lakh twenty five thousand five hundred

   d. Forty crore fourteen

   e. Thirteen crore, twenty lakh five thousand

Expanded Form

Larger numbers are also expanded like the 5-digit numbers.

3,42,65,179 = 30000000 + 4000000 + 200000 + 60000 + 5000 + 100 + 70 + 9

Similarly

2040206 = 2000000 + 40000 + 200 + 6

Comparing Numbers

While comparing large numbers, we compare the number of digits.

The number which has greater number of digits is larger.

If the two numbers have the same number of digits then we start by comparing the leftmost digit. If these are also same, we compare the next digit on the right, and so on.

EXAMPLE

Compare 46589721 and 43979806. Both are 8-digit numbers. Since the leftmost digits are same, compare next digits.

$6 > 3 \therefore 46589721 > 43979806$

Exercise 2.2

1. Write in the expanded form

   a. 88000130

   b. 71134011

   c. 16538427

   d. 4640440

2. Write in the standard form

   a. 10000000 + 10

   b. 60000000 + 7000000 + 400000 + 50000 + 8000 + 20 + 1

   c. 5000000 + 900000 + 30000 + 2000 + 700 + 80 + 1

   d. 70000000 + 7000 + 70

3. Compare the numbers and fill in with '>' or '<'

   a. 12345678 ☐ 12345768   b. 10040004 ☐ 10070007

   c. 36363636 ☐ 36363633   d. 6006006 ☐ 60060006

   e. 567345 ☐ 5673045   f. 6783421 ☐ 6873421

   g. 3329567 ☐ 3229567   h. 7890432 ☐ 7809432

4. Write in the descending order

   a. 13936025;13930625; 13903625; 13093625

   b. 5476312; 5476132; 5471632; 5476321

   c. 37965234; 39765234; 36795234; 39672534

   d. 1234567; 3456719; 4671390; 3457619

5. Write in the ascending order
   a. 8787878; 8787888; 8787887; 8787897
   b. 2328561; 2225861; 2197861; 2308651
   c. 18634695; 22700329; 43214598; 90478110
   d. 44688141; 44488141; 46488141; 46488114

6. Fill in the blanks
   a. The largest 7-digit number is ______________
   b. Successor of the largest 8-digit number is ______________
   c. Predecessor of smallest 9-digit number is ______________
   d. Successor of smallest 8-digit number is ______________
   e. 1 crore is the ______________ of 99,99,999

7. Using the following digits only once, write the smallest and the largest numbers that can be formed.
   a. 6, 4, 3, 0, 9, 1
   b. 1, 9, 8, 0, 5, 4, 7
   c. 7, 9, 0, 6, 8
   d. 2, 1, 0, 5, 9, 8, 6

International Place Value System

Number	Millions			Thousands			Ones		
	Hundred Millions	Ten Millions	Millions	Hundred Thousands	Ten Thousand	Thousands	Hundreds	Tens	Ones
38425976		3	8	4	2	5	9	7	6
80304072	8	0	3	0	4	0	5	2	2

1. 38,425,976-Thirty eight million, four hundred twenty five thousand, nine hundred seventy six
2. 803,040,572-Eight hundred three million forty thousand, five hundred and seventy two.

Exercise 2.3

1. Read the number and write the number name in the International System

   a. 600435070
   b. 945367008
   c. 200012001
   d. 22222222
   e. 702702702
   f. 600001003
   g. 3800000
   h. 403000015

2. Mark the periods and write the place value of underlined digits according to the International System.

   a. 2,8$\underline{8}$8,886
   b. 57,$\underline{8}$88,500
   c. 9$\underline{3}$,084,905
   d. 345,6$\underline{7}$8,921
   e. 30$\underline{6}$00127
   f. 35,68$\underline{3}$,574
   g. 8,0$\underline{0}$0,310
   h. $\underline{1}$29,400,000

3. Make a place value chart of the International System and write the numeral for the following number names.

   a. Seventy million thirty thousand ninety
   b. Eighty eight million two hundred
   c. Three million three thousand three
   d. Four hundred forty million, four hundred four thousand and four
   e. Five hundred million, sixty five thousands, two hundred thirty six

4. Fill in the blanks

	International System	Indian System
1.	One million	10 Lakh
2.		1 Lakh
3.	Hundred million	
4.		100 Lakhs

5. Fill in the boxes with ‘<’ or ‘<’ or ‘=’

a. 30,68,13,723 ☐ 306,813,723

b. 16,543,927 ☐ 1,65,43,972

c. 30,00,000 ☐ 33,000,000

d. Ninety nine lakh ☐ nine hundred thousands

6. Given below is the population of some cities. Write the population, in ascending order, with the name of the city along side:

Chennai	–	4343645	Kolkata	–	4572876
Delhi	–	9879172	Mumbai	–	11978450
Bangaluru	–	4301326	Pune	–	2538473
Hyderabad	–	3637483	Lucknow	–	2185927

Basic Operations

Addition and Subtraction

You are already familiar with addition and subtraction of 5-digit and 6-digit numbers. Large numbers are also added and subtracted in the same way.

Exercise 2.4

1. Addition

a.

	6845396
+	13256978
+	9830

b.

	299278
+	5462036
+	3712493

c.

	63279
+	48001
+	362558

d.

	4076853
+	1785532
+	986671

e.

	5764389
+	23846004
+	13980495

f.

	8974568
+	6468457
+	13000669

2. Write the number which is

a. 15000 more than 1,629,423

b. 8000 more than 41,67,400

c. 3 million more than 12,494

d. 20 Lakhs more than 1,80,47,096

e. 6,00,00,000 more than 18 crores.

3. Subtract

a. 36984 from 130432

b. 572498 from 6354817

c. 702123 from 6043424

d. 2635845 from 10101010

e. 699999 from 800000

4. Fill in the missing digits.

a.

	8	0	7	0	4	2	5	3
+		9	□	5	2	□	4	□
+		□	6	7	□	8	5	2
	□	4	8	□	9	4	□	1

b.

	2	□	6	□	0	□
+		3	4	9	□	5
+	□	9	5	6	7	0
	9	3	□	8	9	6

c.

	2	6	5	□	9	6
+	1	□	4	6	3	□
	□	2	□	4	□	3

d.

	9	□	7	4	□	□	5
−	□	9	4	□	7	3	□
	2	3	3	0	0	4	2

e.

	6	2	□	4	□	2
−	□	□	5	□	7	□
	3	2	4	7	3	2

f.

	4	0	0	0	0	0	0	0
−		2	□	4	6	2	□	1	□
		□	3	□	□	7	4	□	6

Word Problems

Solve the following problems

a. Sum of two numbers is 4,37,986. If the smaller number is 69,219 find the larger number.

b. In a lottery Mr. Parekh won ₹ 1,00,00,000. He spent ₹ 30,50,500 on a flat, ₹ 28,49,980 on a car and deposited the rest in a bank. How much did he deposit in the Bank?

c. By how much in 6,84,30,000 greater than 5,39,86,796?

d. By how much is 17,14,454 less than 19,19,971?

Multiplication

Let us recall the properties of multiplication that we have learnt.

1. When two numbers are multiplied, we get the **product**.
2. The product does not change if the order of the numbers multiplied is changed.
3. Product of any number and zero is always 0.
4. Any number × 1 = number itself.
5. Product of 3 numbers does not change when the grouping of numbers is changed.
6. When a number is multiplied by 10, the product is the no. with a '0' on its right.

   Example: 238 × 10 = 2380
7. Similarity, number × 100 = number with two zeros on its right. 4398 × 100 = 439800

Exercise 2.5

1. Find the product

   a. 8654 × 78
   b. 26857 × 89
   c. 6975 × 935
   d. 32689 × 126
   e. 3943 × 2164
   f. 7358 × 1460
   g. 198547 × 362
   h. 4873 × 1065
   i. 5976 × 654
   j. 4912 × 1475

2. Solve the given word problems

   a. Cost of a bicycle is ₹ 4350. Find the cost of 225 such bicycles.

   b. A truck can carry 5450 kg of goods. How much can 650 such trucks carry?

   c. A sugar factory produces 3450 kg of sugar in a day. How much sugar will be produced in a year?

   d. In a school there are 1869 children. To raise a fund for flood relief each child contributes ₹ 250. How much money will be raised for the flood relief?

   e. A man earns ₹ 23,350 per month. How much will be earn in 6 years?

   f. Cost of 1 box of crayons is ₹ 24. Find the cost of 12150 such boxes.

EXAMPLE

Find the product 5347 and 286

5347		
× 286	→	200 + 80 + 6
32082	→	(5347 × 6)
427760	→	(5347 × 80)
1069400	→	(5347 × 200)
1529242	→	(5347 × 286)

EXAMPLE

Find the product 9896 and 1437

9896
× 1437
______

Division

Repeated subtraction of a number from a given number is division. Equal distribution of a given quantity is division.

Division by zero is not possible.

Dividend = Quotient × Divisor + Remainder

Exercise 2. 6

1. Divide and check

   a. 28364 ÷ 39 b. 51972 ÷ 124

   c. 685432 ÷ 265 d. 659241 ÷ 700

   e. 49261 ÷ 500 f. 74236 ÷ 6000

   g. 501666 ÷ 515 h. 1789625 ÷ 372

2. Think and solve

   a. Cost of 1 bag is ₹ 950. How many bags can be bought for ₹ 85,500?

b. Product of 165 and a number is 120450. Find the number.

c. Cost of a toy gun is ₹ 86. How many such guns can be bought for ₹ 3000?

d. Eggs were packed in boxes that hold 144 eggs each. If a poultry farm needs to pack 12, 41, 856 eggs, how many such boxes would be needed?

e. Find the quotient and remainder when the greatest 5-digit number made with digits 6, 8, 9, 0, 2 is divided by the smallest 3-digit number with digits 6, 8, 2

f. Find the largest 7-digit number divisible by 2334.

Roman Numbers

There are 7 basic Roman Numbers.

Roman Number	I	V	X	L	C	D	M
Hindi Arabic	1	5	10	50	100	500	1000

By combining the above letters, Romans formed different numbers.

Rules

1. Repetition is addition
2. V, L, D can't be repeated
3. No numeral can be repeated for more than 3 times
4. Smaller numeral written to right of a larger numeral is always added to the larger numeral
5. Smaller numeral written to left of the larger numeral is always subtracted from the larger
6. X can only be subtracted from L and C
7. I can be subtracted from X and V only

When we write Roman numerals up to 100, we separate the tens and ones. We first write the Roman numeral (s) for the tens, then for the ones on its right.

EXAMPLE

54 = 50 + 4 = LIV

68 = 60 + 8 = LXVIII

97 = 90 + 7 = XCVII

LXXII = 72

Exercise 2.7

1. Circle the correct Roman numbers.

a. 46	LXVI	XLVI	VILX
b. 53	LIII	XLXIII	LIV
c. 85	LVXXX	XXCV	LXXXV
d. 65	LVX	LXV	VIV
e. 69	LXIX	LXXI	VIIX
f. 92	XCII	LXXXXII	XXCXII

2. Write the Hindu Arabic numerals corresponding to

a. LIV	b. XCV
c. LIX	d. XLV
e. XCIV	f. XLIX
g. XCIX	h. XCII

Larger Roman Numbers

CM is 1000 – 100 = 900

MCM is 1000 + 900 = 1900

1965 is MCMLXV

So, what is MCDXCV?

MCDXCV is 1000 + 400 + 90 + 5 = 1495

Exercise 2. 8

1. Write the Roman Numerals for

   a. 1550 b. 1885 c. 1482

   d. 2010 e. 2760 f. 295

2. Write the Hindu Arabic numeral for

   a. MCMV b. MDCLXX c. MMCCXIX d. DCCXLVII

3. Fill in the blanks with Roman numerals.

   a. I was born in the year ________

   b. India became independent in the year ________

   c. Indira Gandhi was born in the year ________

   d. For the first time man stepped on the moon in the year ________

   e. Wright Brothers made the first aeroplane in the year ________

Mental Maths

1. 9999 + 99 + 9 = __________
2. Predecessor of the smallest 7-digit number is __________
3. Successor of 1 crore is __________
4. 2 million more than 1,99,30,419 is __________
5. 1,000,000 is the successor of __________
6. The difference between 672 and the number obtained by reversing the digits is __________
7. The smallest 6-digit number using different digits is __________
8. The greatest 6-digit number using different digits is __________
9. 1 crore = __________ millions
10. The successor of 610599 is __________

3 Multiples and Factors

Let us take a quick look at what we studied in class 4

$6 \times 1 = 6$ $6 \times 2 = 12$ $6 \times 3 = 18$ $6 \times 4 = 24$

6, 12, 18, 24 are the first 4 multiples of 6

If $6 \times 1 = 6$ then $\frac{6}{1} = 6$ and $\frac{6}{6} = 1$

Similarly $6 \times 2 = 12$ then $\frac{12}{6} = 2$, $\frac{12}{2} = 6$

- A number is a multiple of another number when it is exactly divisible by the other number.
- A multiple of a number = the number × a counting number.
- A number is a multiple of itself.
- All numbers are multiples of 1.

Factors

Factors of a number divide the number without leaving any remainder.

Hence $6 \times 4 = 24$

Then $24 \div 6 = 4$ and $24 \div 4 = 6$

Factors of 24 are 4 and 6

24 is a multiple of 4 and 6.

Prime Numbers

Prime numbers are those numbers which have only 2 factors, 1 and the number itself.

Example: 2, 3, 5, 7,11,13,17,19 etc.

Composite numbers have more than 2 factors.

4, 6, 8, 9, 10, 12, 14, 15, 16, 18, 20 etc.

1 is neither prime nor composite.

- A number is a factor of itself.
- 1 is a factor of every number.

Prime Factors : Factors of a number which are prime, are called **prime factors**.

Example: Factors of 24 are 1, 2, 3, 4, 6, 8, 12, 24 Prime factors are 2, 3

Every number can be written as a product of its prime factors. This is prime factorization of a number.

EXAMPLE

Write the Prime factorisation of the following numbers 36, 48, 54

a. $36 = 2 \times 18 = 2 \times 2 \times 9 = 2 \times 2 \times 3 \times 3$

b. $48 = 2 \times 24 = 2 \times 2 \times 12 = 2 \times 2 \times 2 \times 6 = 2 \times 2 \times 2 \times 2 \times 3$

c. $54 = 2 \times 27 = 2 \times 3 \times 9 = 2 \times 3 \times 3 \times 3$

Prime factors can also be found by repeated division by prime numbers.

EXAMPLE

a. Find the prime factors of 40.

Divide first by 2. Go on dividing until the quotient is not divisible by 2. Then divide by the next prime number.

Go on till the quotient is a prime number

$40 = 2 \times 2 \times 2 \times 5$

2	40
2	20
2	10
2	5

b. Prime factors of 48

$48 = 2 \times 2 \times 2 \times 2 \times 3$

2	48
2	24
2	12
2	6
2	3

Factor Tree

Prime factors can also be found by factorizing in a form called factor free.

Find prime factors of 60.

So, prime factorisation of

$60 = 2 \times 2 \times 3 \times 5$

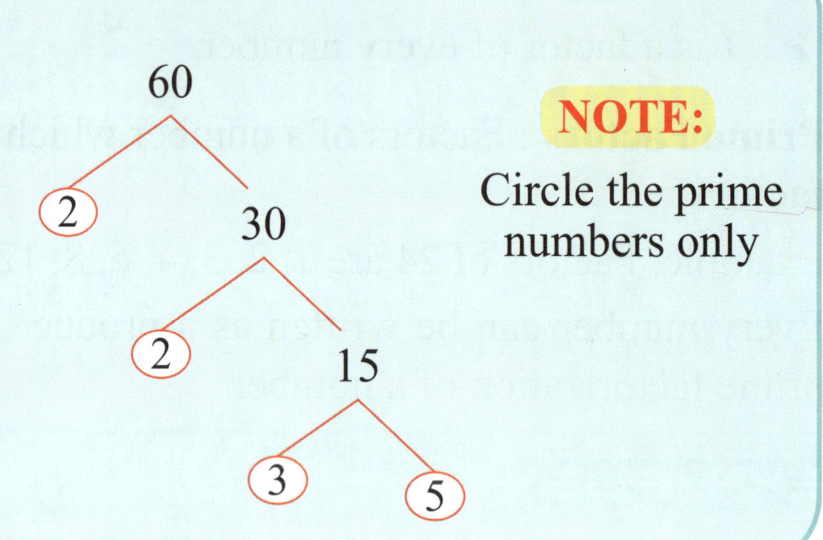

Exercise 3.1

1. Find prime factors of

   a. 36   b. 56   c. 64.   d. 75

   e. 100   f. 112   g. 120   h. 160

2. Draw a factor tree of

   a. 72   b. 128   c. 48   d. 42

3. Write all the prime numbers lying between-2 and 20; 21 and 40; 41 and 60; 61 to 80; 81 to 100;

4. Write all composite numbers lying between 1 to 40; 41 to 90 and 91 to 100.

Highest Common Factor or HCF

Let us take 2 composite numbers 16 and 24.

Factors 16: (1), (2), (4), (8), 16

Factors 24: (1), (2), 3, (4), 6, (8), 12, 24

The circled numbers 1, 2, 4, 8 are common factors.

8 the highest and thus the HCF of 16 and 24.

HCF by Prime factorization

EXAMPLE

Let us find, HCF of 28 and 32 by prime factorization.

Prime factors of 28 = $\boxed{2} \times \boxed{2} \times 7$

Prime factors of 32 = $\boxed{2} \times \boxed{2} \times 2 \times 3$

Common factors are 2, 2

HCF = 2×2 (product of common factors)

EXAMPLE

HCF of 18 and 81

Prime factors of 18 = $2 \times \boxed{3} \times \boxed{3}$

Prime factors of 81 = $3 \times \boxed{3} \times \boxed{3} \times 3$

Common factors = 3, 3

HCF $3 \times 3 = 9$

HCF by common division method of prime factorisation

2	56, 64
2	28, 32
2	14, 16
	7, 8

First divide the numbers by the smallest possible prime number write the quotient below.

Now divide these quotients by the smallest prime number again. Repeat the step, See if there is any more common prime number to divide the quotients stop division if there is no common prime number to divide the quotients.

common factors 2, 2, 2

HCF of 56, 64 is the product of all common factors, $2 \times 2 \times 2 = 8$

EXAMPLE

Find the HCF of 13, 35, 24

1	13, 35, 24
	13, 35, 24

There is no possible common prime factor to divide all the numbers. The only common factor is 1. Thus, HCF of the numbers is 1.

HCF by long division method

To find HCF of larger numbers, prime factorization method becomes difficult. In such cases, we use the LONG DIVISION method.

EXAMPLE

Find HCF of 120 and 440

1. Divide the larger number by the smaller number
2. We get Q = 3; R = 80
3. The remainder becomes divisor and 1st divisor is the dividend
4. Repeat the above step and go on till we get remainder = 0
5. The last divisor is the HCF of the numbers

```
      3
120)440 (3
   -360
   ----
     80) 120 (1
         -80
         ---
          40 ) 80 (2
              -80
              ---
               X
```

HCF of 120 and 440 is 40

EXAMPLE

Find HCF of 90 and 73 follow the above steps.

```
73)90(1
   -73
   17)73(4
      -68
       5)17(3
         -15
          2)5(2
            -4
            1)2(2
              -2
               0
```

HCF of 90 & 73 ⟶ 1

Interesting!

1. If HCF of 2 numbers is 1, they are called **co-primes**
   Example: 2, 7; 3, 5; 10, 11
2. All consecutive numbers are co-primes.

Exercise 3.2

1. Find HCF of the following numbers by prime factorization method.

a. 30 and 96
b. 54 and 162
c. 44 and 88
d. 98 and 154
e. 105, 84 and 42
f. 120 and 96
g. 28, 56 and 84
h. 50 and 58

2. Find the HCF of the following numbers by long division method.

a. 70 and 187
b. 98 and 154
c. 180 and 450
d. 544 and 816
e. 380 and 418
f. 300 and 396
g. 690 and 960
h. 722 and 1406

Least Common Multiple (LCM)

Let us list multiples of 8 and 12

Multiples of 8 are 8, 16, 24, 32, 40, 48, 56, 64, 72, 80

Multiples of 12 are 12, 24, 36, 48, 60, 72, 84, 96

The common multiples are 24, 48 and 72

24 is the smallest and is called the **least common multiples (LCM)** of 8 and 12

This method is not always helpful.

Finding LCM by prime factorization.

EXAMPLE

Find LCM of 12 and 30

Prime factors of 12 = $2 \times 2 \times 3$

Prime factors of 30 = $2 \times 3 \times 5$

To find LCM of 12 and 30, write the common factors first and then the factors that are left out.

LCM of 12 and 30 = 2×3 (Common factors) $\times$ 2×5 (factors that are left)

= 60

2	12
2	6
3	3
	1

2	30
3	15
5	5
	1

EXAMPLE

Find LCM of 28 and 32

Prime factors of 28 = 2 × 2 × 7

Prime factors of 32 = 2 × 2 × 2 × 2 × 2

LCM = 2 × 2 × 7 × 2 × 2 × 2

= 224

2	28
2	14
7	7
	1

2	32
2	16
2	8
2	4
2	2
	1

There is another method called the **common division method** (and the popular method)

EXAMPLE

Find LCM of 18, 36 and 72

1. Start dividing the numbers by the smallest prime number that divides at least 2 of them.
2. Write the quotients and go on dividing till the last row has only prime numbers.

2	18, 36, 72
2	9, 18, 36
3	9, 9, 18
3	3, 3, 6
	1, 1, 2

Now multiply these numbers for LCM

LCM = 2 × 2 × 3 × 3 × 2 = 72

EXAMPLE

Find the LCM of 15, 25, 30

3	15, 25, 30
5	5, 25, 10
	1, 5, 2

LCM = 3 × 5 × 5 × 2 = 150

Remember

If the numbers are multiples of the smallest number, then greatest number is the LCM and smallest number is HCF.

Exercise 3. 3

1. Find LCM by prime factorization method.

   a. 60, 85 b. 16, 32

   c. 18, 27 d. 9, 54

   e. 28, 84 f. 36, 72, 24

2. Find LCM by common division method.

   a. 50, 75 b. 112, 144

   c. 192, 216 d. 105, 150

Relationship between two numbers and their HCF and LCM

Let us make a table as follows.

Numbers	HCF	LCM	Product of numbers	Product of HCF and LCM
6, 8	2	24	$6 \times 8 = 48$	$2 \times 24 = 48$
8, 16	8	16	$8 \times 16 = 128$	$8 \times 16 = 128$
9, 10	1	90	$9 \times 10 = 90$	$1 \times 90 = 90$
12, 16	4	48	$12 \times 16 = 192$	$4 \times 48 = 192$
22, 24	2	264	$22 \times 24 = 528$	$2 \times 264 = 528$

Hence, we can conclude that the product of two numbers is always equal to the product of their LCM and HCF.

Product of numbers = HCF × LCM

EXAMPLE

The product of 2 numbers is 160, if their HCF is 4, find their LCM.

Solution: We know HCF × LCM = Product

$4 \times \boxed{\text{LCM}} = 160$

$\boxed{\text{LCM}} = 160 \div 4$

So, $\boxed{\text{LCM}} = 40$

Remember

Every multiplication fact has 2 division facts!

EXAMPLE

The product of HCF and LCM of 2 numbers is 528. If one of the numbers is 22, find the other number

We know product of 2 numbers = HCF × LCM

1st number × 2nd number = 528

22 × (2nd number) = 528

2nd number = 528 ÷ 22 = 24

Answer: Hence the 2nd number is 24

Therefore we can say,

1. LCM = Product of numbers ÷ HCF
2. HCF = Product of numbers ÷ LCM
3. 1st number × 2nd number = HCF × LCM
4. 2nd number = $\dfrac{\text{HCF} \times \text{LCM}}{(1^{st}\text{ number})}$

Exercise 3.4

1. Complete the table

Numbers	Product	HCF	LCM
8, 30	240	2	______
32, 36	1152	4	______
	612		68

2. Write the missing numbers-

a. 36, ☐ 36 = ___ × ___ × 3 × 3

☐ = ___ × ___ × 7

LCM = ___ × ___ × 3 × 3 × 7 = ___

b. 39, 26 39 = 3 × ___

26 = 2 × ___

LCM = ___ × 3 × 2

3. HCF of 2 numbers is 12 and their LCM is 144. If one number is 36, find the 2nd number.

4. If product of 2 number is 756 and their HCF is 6, find their LCM?

5. LCM and HCF of 2 number is 2310 and 33 respectively. If one of the numbers is 231, find the second number.

Tests of Divisibility

In class IV you had studied that all even numbers are divisible by 2

1. It means when any even number is divided by 2, the remainder is 0.

   So, any number (3-digit or 7-digit or 8-digit) ending in 0, 2, 4, 6, 8 is divisible by 2.

2. Any number is divisible by 5 if it has 0 or 5 in its ones place.

   1280 and 4735 are divisible by 5 and 6762; 13006 are not divisible by 5.

3. Any number is divisible by 10 if it has 0 in its ones place; Eg- 3700; 69020 are divisible by 10 and 555001 and 7611 are not divisible by 10.

4. **Test of divisibility for 3**

   If the sum of the digits in a number is divisible by 30, then the number is divisible by 3.

EXAMPLE

747 in divisible by 3 as 7 + 4 + 7 = 18 is divisible by 3. 436 is not divisible as 4 + 3 + 6 = 13 is not divisible by 3.

5. **Test of divisibility for 4**

   The number formed by the digits in tens and ones place of the given number is divisible by 4 (the last 2-digit) 6352 is divisible by 4 as 52 is divisible by 4. 7843 is not divisible as 43 is not divisible by 4.

6. **Test of divisibility for 9**

   A number is divisible by 9. If sum of the digits of the number is divisibly by 9.

7. Test of divisibility for 6

Any number is divisible by 6 if it is divisible by both 2 and 3.

EXAMPLE

The number126 is an even number, hence divisible by 2.

1 + 2 + 6 = 9 is divisible by 3. So, 126 in divisible by both 2 and 3. Hence, 126 are divisible by 6.

Exercise 3.5

1. Check for divisibility for 2, 3, 4, 5, 6, 9 and 10.

   Put a (✓) for divisible and (×) for not divisible.

Number	2	3	4	5	6	9	10
84							
919							
2340							
5475							
66660							

4 Fractions

Let us revise what have we learnt in previous classes.

←Equivalent Fractions →

$\frac{1}{2}$ $\frac{2}{4}$

$$\frac{1}{2} = \frac{1 \times 2}{2 \times 2} = \frac{2}{4}$$

$$\frac{1}{2} = \frac{1 \times 3}{2 \times 3} = \frac{3}{6}$$

Types of Fractions

Like and Unlike fractions

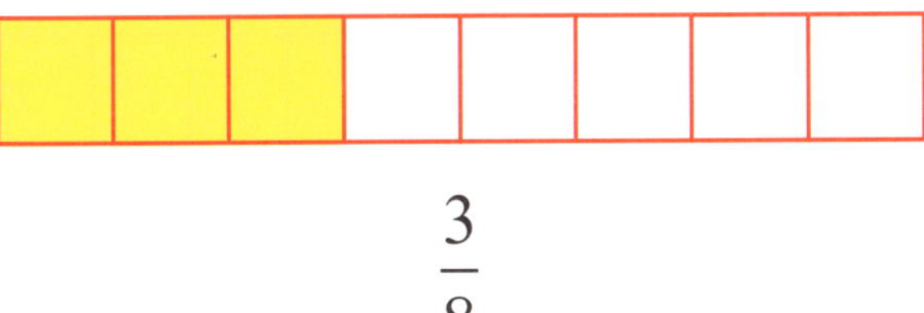

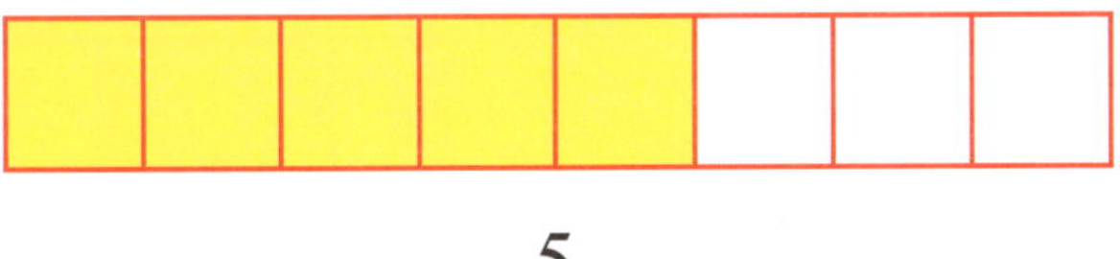

$\frac{3}{8}$ $\frac{5}{8}$

If denominators of both fractions are same they are called **like fractions**

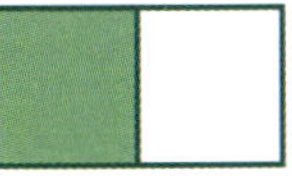

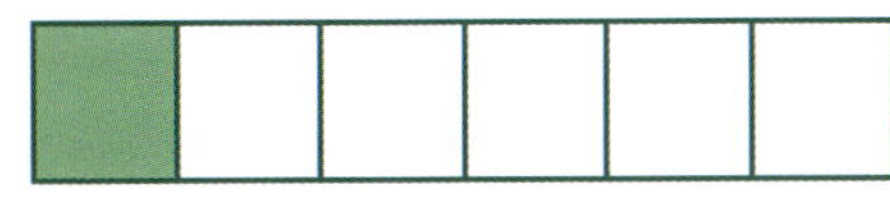

$\frac{1}{2}$ $\frac{1}{6}$

If denominators of both fractions are different, they are **unlike** fractions.

Comparison of Like Fractions

While comparing like fractions compare only the numerators.

So, $\frac{2}{7}$ and $\frac{5}{7}$

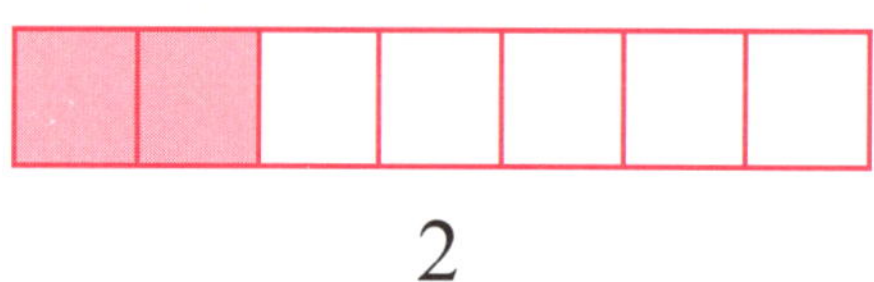

$$\frac{2}{7} < \frac{5}{7}$$

EXAMPLE

Compare $\frac{13}{25}$ and $\frac{18}{25}$

$$\frac{13}{25} < \frac{18}{25}$$

Addition and subtraction of Like Fractions

Add

$\frac{3}{7} + \frac{1}{7}$

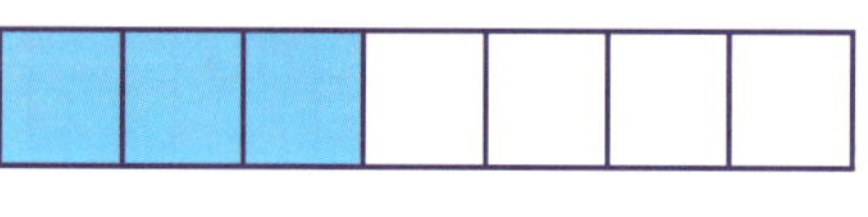

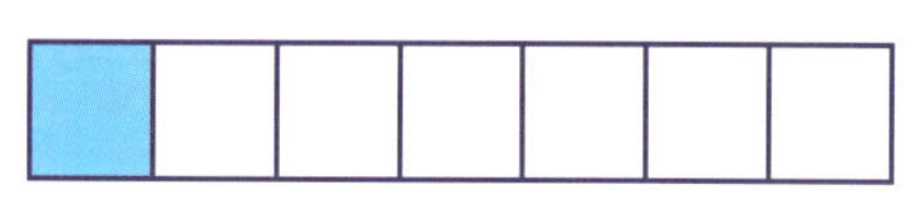

$\frac{3}{7}$ $\frac{1}{7}$

$= \frac{3+1}{7} = \frac{4}{7}$

- Add the numerators
- Write down the same denominator

EXAMPLE

Add $\frac{4}{15}$ and $\frac{5}{15}$

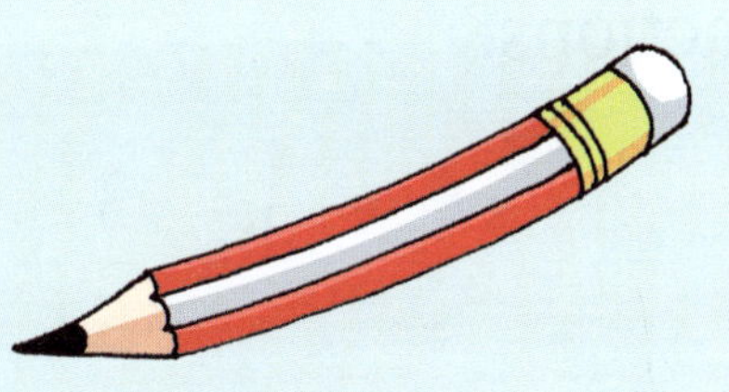

Solution $\frac{4+5}{15} = \frac{9}{15}$

Subtraction of Like Fractions

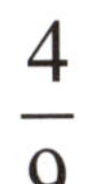

$\frac{1}{9}$

$= \frac{4-1}{9}$

$= \frac{3}{9}$

- Subtract the numerators
- Write down the same denominator

EXAMPLE

Subtract $\frac{9}{10} - \frac{2}{10}$

$\frac{9-2}{10} = \frac{7}{10}$

Exercise 4.1

1. Add the fractions.

a. $\frac{1}{4}+\frac{1}{4}$ b. $\frac{3}{5}+\frac{1}{5}$ c. $\frac{5}{9}+\frac{2}{9}$

2. Subtract the fractions.

a. $\frac{7}{9}-\frac{3}{9}$ b. $\frac{6}{11}-\frac{4}{11}$ c. $\frac{7}{5}-\frac{5}{5}$

More types of fractions

Proper Fractions are those fractions where numerator is less than its denominator.

e.g :- $\frac{1}{4}, \frac{6}{13}, \frac{11}{18}$ are proper fractions.

Improper Fractions are those in which the numerator is greater than or equal to the denominator.

e.g :- $\frac{7}{4}, \frac{8}{3}, \frac{11}{11}, \frac{18}{10}$ are improper fractions.

Unit Fraction is that fraction whose numerator is 1.

e.g :- $\frac{1}{2}, \frac{1}{5}, \frac{1}{10}$ are unit fractions.

Mixed Fraction

2 biscuits + $\frac{1}{2}$ biscuit is $2 + \frac{1}{2}$ or $2\frac{1}{2}$ which is a mixed fraction.

Whenever a whole number is combined with a proper fraction, we get a **mixed fraction**.

$$3 + \frac{1}{4} = 3\frac{1}{4}$$

$$1 + \frac{1}{3} = 1\frac{1}{3}$$

Exercise 4.2

1. Identify the proper fraction and circle them.

   a. $\frac{2}{7}$ b. $\frac{8}{5}$ c. $\frac{5}{8}$ d. $\frac{16}{18}$ e. $\frac{22}{20}$ f. $\frac{19}{17}$ g. $\frac{17}{19}$ h. $\frac{10}{11}$

2. Identify the improper fraction and circle them.

   a. $\frac{7}{9}$ b. $\frac{9}{5}$ c. $\frac{4}{5}$ d. $\frac{97}{100}$ e. $\frac{14}{11}$ f. $\frac{16}{35}$ g. $\frac{19}{3}$ h. $\frac{14}{13}$

Conversion of improper fractions into mixed numbers

Convert $\frac{7}{3}$ into a mixed number.

Solution $\frac{7}{3} = 7 \div 3$

$\frac{7}{3} = 2\frac{1}{3}$

$3\overline{)7}(2$ ← Quotient

$\underline{6}$

1 ← Remainder

(check 3×2+1=7 numerator of improper fraction)

EXAMPLE

Convert $\frac{8}{5}$ to a mixed number.

Solution $\frac{8}{5} = 8 \div 5 =$

$\frac{8}{5} = 1\frac{3}{5}$

$5\overline{)8}(1$

$\underline{5}$

3

(check $5 \times 1 + 3 = 8$ is the numerator of improper fraction)

Conversion of mixed number into an improper fraction

EXAMPLE

Convert $1\frac{2}{3}$ into a improper fractions

$1 = \frac{3}{3}$

Solution $1\frac{2}{3} = 1 + \frac{2}{3} \quad = \frac{3}{3} + \frac{2}{3} \quad = \frac{5}{3}$

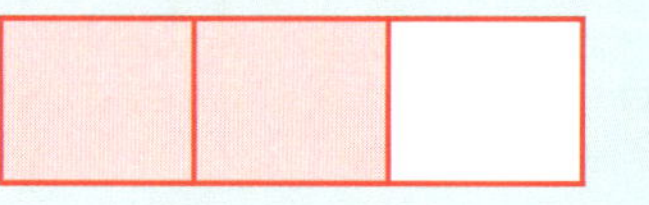

$\frac{2}{3}$

Alternate Method

$1\frac{2}{3}$ is $3 \times 1 + 2$ (Multiply denominator 3 by the whole number 1 and add numerator to the product)

$= \frac{5}{3}$

This is the shorter method.

EXAMPLE

Convert $4\frac{1}{5}$ into a improper fractions

Solution $\frac{5 \text{x} 4}{5} = 20$

$20 + 1 = 21$

$4\frac{1}{5} = \frac{21}{5}$

Exercise 4.3

1. Fill in the boxes.

a. $\frac{7}{2} = 3\frac{\square}{2}$

b. $\frac{9}{2} = \square\frac{1}{2}$

c. $4\frac{3}{5} = \frac{\square}{5}$

d. $6\frac{1}{7} = \frac{43}{\square}$

e. $9\frac{1}{9} = \frac{\square}{9}$

f. $\frac{12}{5} = \square\frac{\square}{5}$

g. $2\frac{19}{20} = \frac{\square}{\square}$

h. $\frac{22}{3} = \square\frac{\square}{\square}$

2. Convert the following fraction into mixed numbers.

a. $\frac{11}{4}$ b. $\frac{20}{7}$ c. $\frac{31}{3}$ d. $\frac{28}{9}$

e. $\frac{25}{8}$ f. $\frac{13}{9}$ g. $\frac{14}{5}$ h. $\frac{19}{6}$

3. Convert the following mixed numbers to improper fractions.

a. $5\frac{1}{6}$ b. $6\frac{1}{2}$ c. $3\frac{4}{7}$ d. $4\frac{1}{12}$

e. $2\frac{4}{11}$ f. $5\frac{7}{10}$ g. $1\frac{3}{13}$ h. $7\frac{1}{4}$

Lab Activity

For Comparison of Fractions

Take 8 strips of paper (same size)

Look at the coloured part.

What do we see?

$$1 > \frac{1}{2} > \frac{1}{3} > \frac{1}{4} > \frac{1}{5} > \frac{1}{6} > \frac{1}{7} > \frac{1}{9}$$

And so, if two fractions have the same numerator the fractions which has the smaller denominator is greater.

EXAMPLE

Compare $\frac{2}{5}$ and $\frac{2}{7}$

Solution Since numerators are same we look at denominators. The smaller denominator is greater fraction, hence

$$\frac{2}{5} > \frac{2}{7}$$

EXAMPLE

Compare $\frac{7}{9}$ and $\frac{7}{8}$

Solution $\frac{7}{9} < \frac{7}{8}$ (The smaller denominator is the greater fraction)

Comparison of unlike fractions

EXAMPLE

Compare $\frac{2}{5}$ and $\frac{1}{4}$

Solution There has to be something common. To make denominators same we take LCM of 5 and 4. LCM of 5, 4= 20

Write equivalent fractions of $\frac{2}{5}$ and $\frac{1}{4}$ with denominator 20.

$$\frac{2}{5} = \frac{2 \times 4}{5 \times 4} = \frac{8}{20} \qquad \frac{1}{4} = \frac{1 \times 5}{4 \times 5} = \frac{5}{20}$$

$\frac{8}{20} > \frac{5}{20}$ So, $\frac{2}{5} > \frac{1}{4}$

[First we convert them into like fractions and then compare]

EXAMPLE

Compare $\frac{3}{7}$ and $\frac{2}{5}$

Solution LCM of 7, 5 =35

$$\frac{3}{7} = \frac{3 \text{x} 5}{7 \text{x} 5} = \frac{15}{35}$$

$$\frac{2}{5} = \frac{2 \text{x} 7}{5 \text{x} 7} = \frac{14}{35}$$

$$\frac{15}{35} > \frac{14}{35}$$

$$\frac{3}{7} > \frac{2}{5}$$

EXAMPLE

Compare $4\frac{1}{2}$ and $\frac{9}{7}$

Solution $4\frac{1}{2} = \frac{9}{2}$ and $\frac{9}{7}$

$$\frac{9}{2} > \frac{9}{7}$$

Exercise 4.4

1. Find the smaller fraction is each pair-

a. $\frac{2}{9}, \frac{7}{9}$ b. $\frac{9}{13}, \frac{4}{13}$ c. $\frac{7}{8}, \frac{1}{8}$ d. $1\frac{3}{5}, \frac{7}{5}$

2. Find the greater fraction in each pair

a. $\frac{5}{6}, \frac{5}{7}$ b. $\frac{7}{10}, \frac{7}{13}$ c. $\frac{1}{3}, \frac{1}{5}$ d. $\frac{8}{15}, \frac{3}{15}$

3. Write in ascending order.

a. $\frac{8}{11}, \frac{9}{11}, \frac{1}{11}, \frac{4}{11}$

b. $\frac{12}{25}, \frac{11}{25}, \frac{13}{25}, \frac{10}{25}, 1\frac{1}{25}$

4. Write in descending order.

a. $\frac{2}{7}, \frac{2}{5}, \frac{2}{11}, \frac{2}{8}$

b. $\frac{10}{19}, \frac{10}{17}, \frac{10}{11}, \frac{10}{21}$

Writing a fraction in lowest form

EXAMPLE

Write $\frac{10}{12}$ in its lowest form

To express a fraction in its lowest form follow these steps:

1. Find common factor of numerator and denominator

2. Then $\frac{\text{Num.} \div \text{Common factor}}{\text{Denom.} \div \text{Common factor}}$ = Fraction in lowest from

Common factor of 10, 12 is 2

$\frac{10 \div 2}{12 \div 2} = \frac{5}{6}$ **Answer**

EXAMPLE

Express $\frac{18}{24}$ in its lowest form.

Common factors of 18 and 24 are 2, 3, 6

Choose the HCF i.e. 6

$\frac{18 \div 6}{24 \div 6} = \frac{3}{4}$ or we can do like this $\frac{18 \div 2}{24 \div 2} = \frac{9}{12}$ this can be further reduced to

$\frac{9 \div 3}{12 \div 3} = \frac{3}{4}$

Note: You would see cancellation of this type. $\frac{\cancel{18}^{\cancel{9}}}{\cancel{24}_{\cancel{12}}}$ $\frac{3}{4}$

This can be achieved with practice.

Addition of Unlike Fractions

We had learnt addition of like fractions previously.

Now let's learn addition of unlike fractions

EXAMPLE

Add $\frac{1}{5}$ and $\frac{2}{3}$

Solution While comparing fractions we took LCM of denominators, to convert them into like fractions. LCM of 5 and 3 is 15.

$\frac{1}{5} = \frac{1 \times 3}{5 \times 3} = \frac{3}{15}$ $\frac{2}{3} = \frac{2 \times 5}{3 \times 5} = \frac{10}{15}$

$\frac{1}{5} + \frac{2}{3} = \frac{3}{15} + \frac{10}{15} = \frac{13}{15}$

EXAMPLE

Add $\frac{3}{4}, \frac{1}{2}, \frac{5}{8}$

LCM of 4, 2, 8 = 8

$\therefore \frac{3}{4} = \frac{3 \text{x} 2}{4 \text{x} 2} = \frac{6}{8}; \frac{1}{2} = \frac{1 \text{x} 4}{2 \text{x} 4} = \frac{4}{8}; \frac{5}{8} = \frac{5}{8}$

$\frac{3}{4} + \frac{1}{2} + \frac{5}{8} = \frac{6}{8} + \frac{4}{8} + \frac{5}{8} = \frac{6+4+5}{8} = \frac{15}{8} = 1\frac{7}{8}$

EXAMPLE

Add $1\frac{3}{8}$ **and** $3\frac{5}{12}$

$1\frac{3}{8} = \frac{11}{8}$ $\quad 3\frac{5}{12} = \frac{41}{12}$

LCM of 8, 12 = 24

$\frac{11}{8} = \frac{11 \text{x} 3}{8 \text{x} 3} = \frac{33}{24}$

$\frac{41}{12} = \frac{41 \text{x} 2}{12 \text{x} 2} = \frac{82}{24}$

$\frac{11}{8} + \frac{41}{12} = \frac{33}{24} + \frac{82}{24}$

$= \frac{115}{24}$

$= 4\frac{19}{24}$ Answer

Exercise 4.5

1. Add the following fractions

a. $\frac{2}{3}+\frac{1}{5}$ b. $\frac{2}{3}+\frac{3}{4}$ c. $\frac{4}{9}+\frac{1}{3}$ d. $\frac{3}{5}+\frac{1}{2}$

e. $\frac{7}{8}+\frac{1}{2}$ f. $\frac{1}{12}+\frac{5}{6}$ g. $\frac{3}{4}+\frac{3}{4}$ h. $\frac{7}{8}+\frac{1}{3}$

i. $\frac{9}{10}+\frac{7}{8}$ j. $\frac{3}{5}+\frac{1}{2}+\frac{1}{3}$ k. $\frac{1}{2}+\frac{3}{4}+\frac{7}{8}$ l. $\frac{1}{4}+\frac{2}{3}+\frac{1}{6}$

2. Add

a. $2\frac{1}{4}+\frac{1}{3}$ b. $8\frac{1}{3}+3\frac{4}{9}$ c. $3\frac{11}{12}+2\frac{5}{6}$ d. $2\frac{7}{19}+8\frac{3}{8}$

e. $3\frac{1}{6}+2\frac{2}{3}$ f. $5\frac{2}{3}+3\frac{4}{7}$ g. $5\frac{7}{8}+2\frac{1}{3}$ h. $4\frac{2}{3}+1\frac{5}{6}+\frac{4}{5}$

i. $3\frac{3}{4}+\frac{9}{10}+2$ j. $3+2\frac{1}{2}+\frac{1}{2}$ k. $2\frac{7}{9}+\frac{8}{5}+3\frac{1}{5}$ l. $\frac{3}{7}+2\frac{5}{6}+3$

Subtraction of Unlike Fractions

For subtraction of unlike fractions also we take LCM

EXAMPLE

Subtract $\frac{3}{7}-\frac{1}{6}$

Solution: LCM of 7, 6 = 42

$\frac{3}{7}=\frac{3x6}{7x6}=\frac{18}{42}$ | $\frac{1}{6}=\frac{1x7}{6x7}=\frac{7}{42}$ | $\frac{3}{7}-\frac{1}{6}=\frac{18}{42}-\frac{7}{42}=\frac{18-7}{42}=\frac{11}{42}$

Answer

EXAMPLE

Subtract $2-\frac{3}{4}$

Solution : LCM of 1, 4 = 4

$$\frac{2}{1}=\frac{2x4}{1x4}=\frac{8}{4} \qquad \frac{3}{4}=\frac{3}{4}$$

$$2-\frac{3}{4}=\frac{8}{4}-\frac{3}{4}=\frac{5}{4} \quad \text{Answer}$$

Exercise 4.6

1. Express in lowest terms.

a. $\frac{21}{42}$ b. $\frac{51}{68}$ c. $\frac{36}{39}$ d. $\frac{45}{54}$

e. $\frac{35}{49}$ f. $\frac{9}{54}$ g. $\frac{20}{35}$ h. $\frac{36}{81}$

2. Subtract

a. $\frac{3}{4}-\frac{5}{12}$ b. $\frac{1}{2}-\frac{3}{8}$ c. $\frac{6}{8}-\frac{3}{4}$ d. $\frac{7}{8}-\frac{1}{3}$

e. $\frac{2}{3}-\frac{5}{12}$ f. $\frac{4}{3}-\frac{5}{6}$ g. $\frac{3}{10}-\frac{1}{4}$ h. $\frac{3}{7}-\frac{3}{10}$

i. $\frac{2}{3}-\frac{5}{11}$ j. $\frac{11}{16}-\frac{5}{8}$ k. $\frac{1}{3}-\frac{1}{4}$ l. $\frac{2}{7}-\frac{2}{9}$

3. Subtract

a. $3\frac{5}{6}-2$ b. $3\frac{4}{9}-2\frac{1}{6}$ c. $7\frac{3}{10}-5\frac{7}{10}$ d. $6\frac{3}{4}-1\frac{2}{8}$

e. $3\frac{7}{8}-2\frac{1}{6}$ f. $4\frac{5}{8}-2\frac{1}{2}$ g. $3\frac{5}{7}-1\frac{4}{9}$ h. $52\frac{1}{4}-50\frac{2}{5}$

i. $8\frac{1}{2}-6\frac{1}{4}$ j. $2\frac{1}{2}-2\frac{1}{4}$ k. $3\frac{5}{8}-2\frac{1}{8}$ l. $5-2\frac{1}{4}$

Word Problems

Hema bought $5\frac{1}{2}$ m of cloth for curtains and $2\frac{1}{4}$ m for sheets. What length of cloth did she buy in all?

Solution Length of cloth bought for curtains = $5\frac{1}{2}$ m

Length of cloth bought for sheets = $2\frac{1}{4}$ m

Total length of cloth bought = $5\frac{1}{2}\text{ m}+2\frac{1}{4}\text{ m}$

$\frac{11}{2}\text{ m}+\frac{9}{4}\text{ m}=\frac{22}{4}+\frac{9}{4}=\frac{31}{4}=7\frac{3}{4}\text{ m}$ Answer

Exercise 4.7

1. Amir jumped $4\frac{1}{3}$ feet. Rahul jumped $1\frac{1}{4}$ feet farther than Amir. How far did Rahul jump?

2. Last year my height was $52\frac{1}{2}$ inches. My height has increased by $1\frac{5}{8}$ inches. How tall am I now?

3. Anita weighs $52\frac{1}{2}$ kg. Ayesha weighs $50\frac{2}{5}$ kg. How much more does Anita weigh?

4. Rita had $4\frac{7}{12}$ m of ribbon. She used $2\frac{1}{5}$ m for decoration. What length of ribbon is left with her?

5. Rohit takes $1\frac{5}{6}$ hours to travel to school. Rekha takes $\frac{1}{2}$ hour more than Rohit. Find the time taken by Rekha (in hours) to reach school.

Multiplication of Fractions

Multiplication is repeated addition. For example,

3 times 4 (is 3×4) = 4 + 4 + 4

Let us see in fractions –

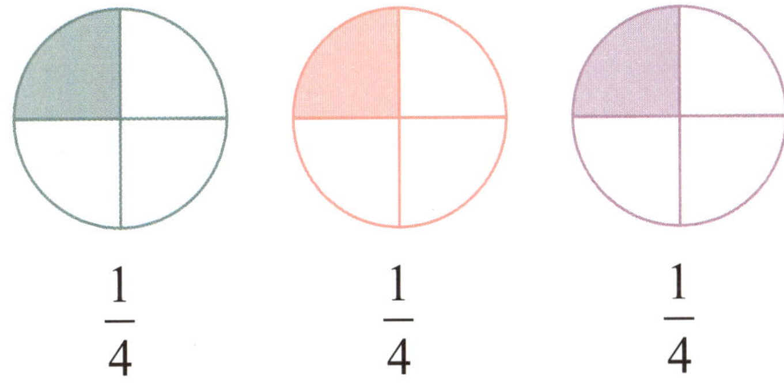

$\frac{1}{4}$ $\frac{1}{4}$ $\frac{1}{4}$

Total shaded portion is $\frac{1}{4}+\frac{1}{4}+\frac{1}{4}=\frac{1+1+1}{4}=\frac{3}{4}$ or $3\text{x}\frac{1}{4}=\frac{3}{4}$

EXAMPLE

Multiplication $2 \times \frac{3}{8}$

 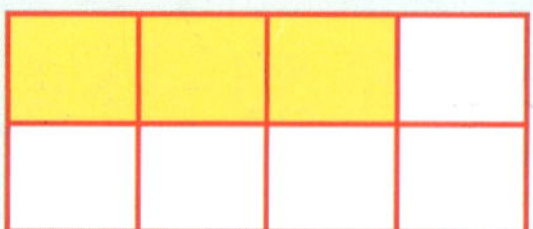

$$\frac{3}{8} + \frac{3}{8}$$

$$2 \times \frac{3}{8} = \frac{6}{8}$$

Simplify further $\frac{6 \div 2}{8 \div 2} = \frac{3}{4}$

Alternately $\frac{\cancel{2}^{1} \times 3}{\cancel{8}_{4}} = \frac{1 \times 3}{4} = \frac{3}{4}$

Multiplication of a fraction by another fraction

EXAMPLE

$\frac{1}{2}$ of $\frac{3}{4}$ is the same as $\frac{1}{2} \times \frac{3}{4} = \frac{1 \times 3}{2 \times 4} = \frac{3}{8}$

EXAMPLE

$\frac{1}{16}$ of $5\frac{1}{3}$ is $\frac{1}{16} \times 5\frac{1}{3}$

$$= \frac{1}{16} \times \frac{16}{3} = \frac{1}{3}$$

$$\text{or } \frac{1}{16} \times \frac{16}{3} = \frac{1 \times 16}{16 \times 3} = \frac{16}{48}$$

$$= \frac{16 \div 4}{48 \div 4} = \frac{4 \div 4}{12 \div 4} = \frac{1}{3}$$

Exercise 4.8

1. Multiply and write in simplest form.

a. $\frac{1}{2}$x10 b. 7x$\frac{4}{5}$ c. $\frac{3}{8}$x16 d. $\frac{3}{4}$x24 e. 0x$\frac{12}{19}$

f. $\frac{9}{19}$x1 g. 6x$\frac{1}{9}$ h. 20x$\frac{2}{5}$ i. $\frac{1}{3}$x8 j. $\frac{1}{8}$x18

2. Multiply and write the product in the simplest form.

a. $\frac{8}{7}$x$\frac{2}{3}$ b. $\frac{2}{5}$x$\frac{1}{3}$ c. $\frac{5}{6}$x$\frac{1}{2}$ d. $\frac{7}{8}$x$\frac{11}{2}$

e. $\frac{8}{15}$x$\frac{3}{2}$ f. $\frac{4}{7}$x$\frac{1}{4}$ g. $\frac{1}{4}$x$\frac{7}{8}$ h. $\frac{5}{12}$x$\frac{16}{30}$

i. $\frac{5}{7}$x$\frac{7}{15}$ j. $\frac{7}{10}$x$\frac{5}{6}$ k. $\frac{6}{13}$x$\frac{13}{30}$ l. $\frac{3}{8}$x$\frac{2}{6}$

m. $\frac{3}{4}$x$\frac{1}{12}$ n. $\frac{7}{8}$x$\frac{4}{21}$ o. $\frac{1}{2}$x$\frac{3}{4}$ p. $\frac{1}{3}$x$4\frac{1}{2}$

q. $\frac{3}{8}$x40 r. $\frac{3}{4}$x$\frac{2}{5}$ s. $\frac{4}{9}$x$\frac{3}{8}$ t. $\frac{15}{49}$x$\frac{14}{45}$

3. Multiply

a. $2\frac{1}{7}$x$\frac{4}{5}$ b. $3\frac{1}{5}$x$\frac{3}{8}$ c. $4\frac{2}{5}$x$\frac{5}{11}$ d. $1\frac{1}{5}$x$2\frac{5}{6}$

e. $3\frac{3}{4}$x$6\frac{2}{5}$ f. $5\frac{2}{3}$x$\frac{7}{17}$ g. $3\frac{3}{4}$x$2\frac{2}{5}$ h. $3\frac{2}{7}$x$\frac{14}{23}$

Reciprocal of fractions

$\frac{1}{2} \times 2 = 1$ $\frac{1}{5} \times 5 = 1$

$\frac{1}{7} \times 7 = 1$ $\frac{1}{11} \times 11 = 1$

$\frac{5}{11} \times \frac{11}{5} = 1$ $\frac{9}{13} \times \frac{13}{9} = 1$

In all the cases shown above we see that the product is 1. When product of two fractions is 1, the two fractions are reciprocal of each other.

So, reciprocal of $\frac{1}{2}$ is 2 and reciprocal of 2 is $\frac{1}{2}$

Reciprocal of $\frac{1}{7}$ is 7 and reciprocal of $\frac{9}{13}$ is $\frac{13}{9}$

Reciprocal of any fraction like $\frac{\text{numerator}}{\text{denominator}}$ is $\frac{\text{denominator}}{\text{numerator}}$

Division

EXAMPLE

Represents 1

Represents $\frac{1}{2}$

Represents $\frac{1}{4}$

we obtain $\frac{1}{4}$ by dividing $\frac{1}{2}$ in to 2 equal parts.

$$\frac{1}{4} = \frac{1}{2} \div 2 \text{ or } \frac{1}{2} \text{ of } \frac{1}{2}$$

$$\frac{1}{2} \div 2 = \frac{1}{2} \text{ of } \frac{1}{2}$$

$$\frac{1}{2} \text{x} \frac{1}{2} = \frac{1}{4}$$

EXAMPLE

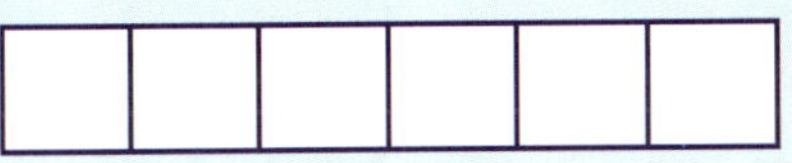

Represents 1

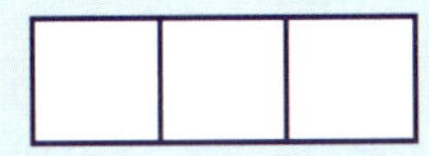

Represents $\frac{1}{3}$

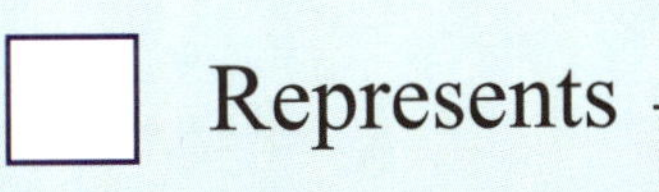

Represents $\frac{1}{4}$

$$\frac{1}{3} \div 2 = \frac{1}{6} = \frac{1}{3} \text{x} \frac{1}{2}$$

we can write $\frac{1}{2} \div 4 = \frac{1}{2} \text{x} \frac{1}{4} = \frac{1}{8}$

EXAMPLE

Divide $\frac{2}{5}$ by 2

$\frac{2}{5} \div 2 = \frac{\cancel{2}^{1}}{5} \times \frac{1}{\cancel{2}_{1}} = \frac{1}{5}$

Division of a whole number by a fraction

EXAMPLE

How many $\frac{1}{3}$ in 1? Ans. 3

Hence there are 3 portions of $\frac{1}{3}$ in 1.

so, $1 \div \frac{1}{3} = 3$

$1 \div \frac{1}{3} = 3$ and $1 \times \frac{3}{1} = 3$

$\left(\frac{3}{1} \text{ is reciprocal of } \frac{1}{3}\right)$

EXAMPLE

How many $\frac{1}{3}$ in 2? Ans. 6

So, since 6 pieces of $\frac{1}{3}$ are in 2,

we write $2 \div \frac{1}{3} = 6$ and $2 \times \frac{3}{1} = 6$

$\left(\frac{3}{1} \text{ is reciprocal of } \frac{1}{3}\right)$

So, a whole number ÷ fraction = whole number × reciprocal of fraction

EXAMPLE

Divide 4 by $\frac{2}{3}$

$$4 \div \frac{2}{3} = \overset{2}{\cancel{4}} \times \frac{3}{\cancel{2}_{1}} = 6$$

So, whole number ÷ fraction = whole number × reciprocal of fraction.

Division of a fraction by a fraction

EXAMPLE

$2\frac{1}{2} \div \frac{1}{4}$

Take a string

$2\frac{1}{2}$ m

$\frac{1}{4}$ m

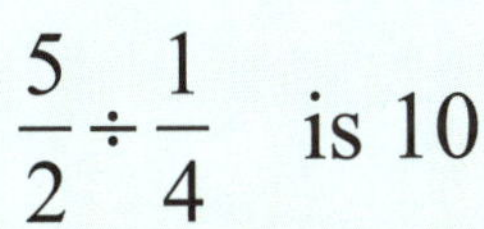

$\frac{5}{2} \div \frac{1}{4}$ is 10

Also, $\frac{5}{2} \times \frac{4}{1} = \frac{\overset{10}{\cancel{20}}}{\cancel{2}_{1}} = 10$

so, $\frac{5}{2} \div \frac{1}{4}$

$= \frac{5}{2} \times 4$

(Fraction 1) ÷ (fraction 2) =

(Fraction 1) × (Reciprocal of fraction 2.)

EXAMPLE

$$3\frac{1}{2} \div \frac{1}{2} = \frac{7}{\cancel{2}_1} \times \frac{\cancel{2}^1}{1} = 7$$

Exercise 4.9

1. Find the reciprocal of

a. $\frac{3}{4}$ b. $\frac{10}{13}$ c. $\frac{1}{9}$ d. $\frac{13}{7}$

e. $2\frac{5}{7}$ f. $3\frac{9}{14}$ g. $4\frac{5}{9}$ h. 1

2. Simplify

a. $10 \div \frac{5}{9}$ b. $4 \div \frac{8}{13}$ c. $15 \div \frac{5}{9}$ d. $12 \div \frac{1}{2}$

e. $5 \div \frac{1}{6}$ f. $6 \div \frac{2}{3}$ g. $8 \div \frac{1}{5}$ h. $51 \div \frac{17}{3}$

e. $12 \div \frac{6}{11}$ f. $\frac{2}{5} \div 2$

3. Simplify the following:

a. $\frac{1}{2} \div \frac{7}{12}$ b. $17 \div \frac{1}{3}$ c. $6 \div \frac{2}{5}$ d. $\frac{4}{5} \div \frac{5}{4}$

e. $4\frac{1}{3} \div \frac{13}{5}$ f. $5\frac{1}{3} \div \frac{13}{5}$ g. $2\frac{4}{5} \div \frac{7}{15}$ h. $3\frac{1}{4} \div \frac{1}{4}$

e. $\frac{9}{28} \div \frac{3}{14}$ f. $\frac{7}{8} \div \frac{21}{16}$

Word problems of multiplication and division

1. In a class there are 42 students. $\frac{4}{7}$ of the students are boys. Find the number of boys and girls.

   Solution: Total number of students = 42

   Number of boys $= \frac{4}{7}$ of 42

   $\frac{\cancel{4}}{\cancel{7}_1} \times \cancel{42}^{6}$

   $= 24$

   Number of girls = 42– 24 = 18 Answer

2. A roll of wire is $2\frac{4}{7}$ m in length. How many pieces of $\frac{3}{7}$ m each can be cut from this roll?

   Solution: Total length of wire $= 2\frac{4}{7}\text{m} = \frac{18}{7}\text{m}$

   Length of each piece $= \frac{3}{7}\text{m}$

   Number of pieces $= 2\frac{4}{7} \div \frac{3}{7}$

   $= \frac{18}{7} \div \frac{3}{7}$

   $= \frac{\cancel{18}^{6}}{\cancel{7}_1} \div \frac{\cancel{7}^{1}}{\cancel{3}_1}$

   $= 6$ Answer

Exercise 4.10

1. $1\frac{1}{2}$ cups of milk are needed to bake 1 cake. How much milk is needed to bake 10 such cakes?

2. If $\frac{3}{4}$ of a number is 60, find the number.

3. How many three fifths are there in 15?

4. By how much is $\frac{3}{4}$ of 184 m more than $\frac{4}{7}$ of 217?

5. Product of $8\frac{2}{5}$ and a fraction is 18. Find the other fraction.

6. A man donates $\frac{1}{8}$ of his salary every month to a Blind school. If he earns ₹ 40,000 per month, find his annual contribution to the blind school.

7. Sheila plays every day for $\frac{3}{4}$ of an hour. Today she spent $\frac{1}{3}$ of this time reading a novel. For how much time did she play?

8. There are 40 students in class VA. $\frac{5}{8}$ of them went to the museum and rest to an Old Age Home. How many went to the Old Age Home?

9. 8 litres of orange juice is poured into glasses. If $\frac{1}{3}$ l is poured into each glass, how many such glasses can be filled?

10. The sale price of a pair of shoes is $\frac{3}{4}$th of the regular price of ₹ 2400. Find the cost at which it was sold during sale period.

Mental Maths

1. State whether the following statements is true or false

   a. $\frac{3}{7}$ and $\frac{6}{21}$ are equivalent fractions

   b. $\frac{9}{1}$ is a proper fraction

   c. $\frac{4}{9}$ and $\frac{4}{13}$ are like fractions.

   d. 15 minutes is one - fourth of an hour.

   e. One - third of 300 is 30.

2. Fill in the blanks

   a. A second is ________ of an hour.

   b. If one fourth of a tank holds 35 litres, then the capacity of the tank is _______l.

   c. _________ is an equivalent fraction of $\frac{4}{5}$

   d. _________ (fraction) of one dozen is 4 eggs.

   e. 12 is one-fourth of a total of ______________

5 Decimal

Study the place value chart

TH	H	T	O	
			1	1
		1	6	$10 = 10 \times 1$
	1	3	4	$100 = 10 \times 10$
1	7	6	2	$1000 = 10 \times 100$

When a digit moves to the left its place value increases by 10. We can also say the place value of a digit becomes one tenth as it moves to the right.

Place value of 1 in 1762 is 1000

Place value of 1 in 134 is $100 = \frac{1}{10} \text{x} 1000$

Place value of 1 in 16 is $10 = \frac{1}{10} \text{x} 10$

Place value of 1 in 1 is $1 = \frac{1}{10} \text{x} 10$

So, when 1 moves right by one place it will be $\frac{1}{10}$ or $1 \div 10$. It is read as one tenth and written as 1 and '.' is the decimal. 0.2 is $\frac{2}{10}$ and read as 'point 2'. 0.7 is $\frac{7}{10}$ and is read as 'point 7'.

The place value chart is extended beyond ones place.

TH	H	T	O	Tenths	
	2	3	6	2	is 236.2

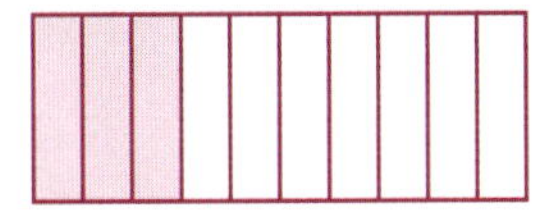

$1 + 1 + \frac{3}{10} = 2.3$

$\frac{5}{10} = 0.5$

Hundredths

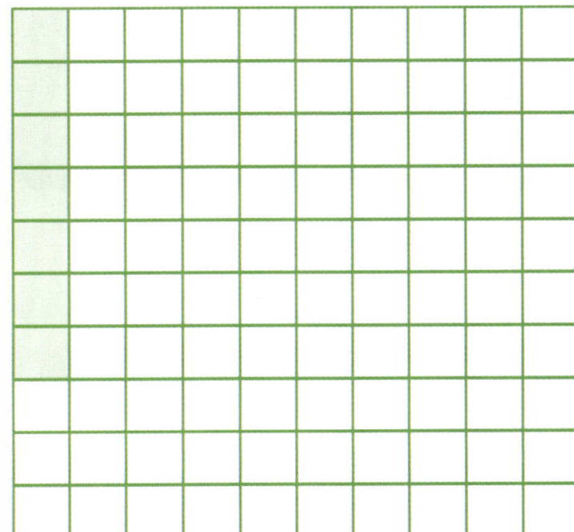

If 10 parts are further divided to 10 equal parts than each part is 1 the hundredth part. Shaded portion is $\frac{7}{100}$ or seven hundredth.

Decimal form is 0.07

1 tenth = 10 hundredth

Thousandths

A fraction with denominator 1000 is called thousandth.

$\frac{5}{1000}$ is five thousandths.

Place value chart

TH	H	T	O	Tenth	Hundredth	Thousandth
	4	3	8	7	9	5
		7	1	6	8	2
			4	2	5	
			6	1		

1. $400 + 30 + 8 + + \frac{7}{10} + \frac{9}{100} + \frac{5}{1000} = 438.795$ [Four hundred and thirty eight point seven nine five]

2. $70 + 1 + \frac{6}{10} + \frac{8}{100} + \frac{2}{1000} = 71.682$ [Seventy one point six eight two]

3. $4 + \frac{2}{10} + \frac{5}{100} = 4.25$ [Four point two five]

4. $6 + \frac{1}{10} = 6.1$ [Six point one]

Exercise 5.1

1. Expand

a. 13.27 b. 48.526 c. 314.6 d. 69.003

e. 9.04 f. 735.264 g. 4.098 h. 10.001

2. Write the decimal number for the following.

a. $20 + \frac{6}{10} + \frac{8}{100}$ b. $300 + \frac{4}{10} + \frac{6}{1000}$

c. $4 + \frac{8}{100} + \frac{4}{1000}$ d. $30 + \frac{3}{100} + \frac{9}{1000}$

e. $42 + \frac{5}{10} + \frac{3}{1000}$ f. $11 + \frac{1}{10} + \frac{1}{100} + \frac{1}{1000}$

g. $24 + 0.4 + 0.01$ h. $0.05 + 0.005$ i. $0.02 + 0.002$

Converting Decimals to Fractions

a. $\frac{8}{10} = 0.8$

b. $\frac{42}{100} = 0.42$

c. $3.6 = 3 + 6x\frac{1}{10}$ or $\frac{36}{10}$

d. $25.34 = \frac{2534}{100}$

Exercise 5.2

1. Write the shaded part in decimals. (First is done for you)

a. 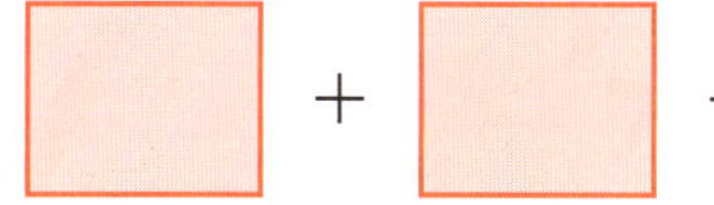 $= 2 + \frac{4}{10} = 2.4$

$1 + 1 + \frac{4}{10} = 0.4$

b. 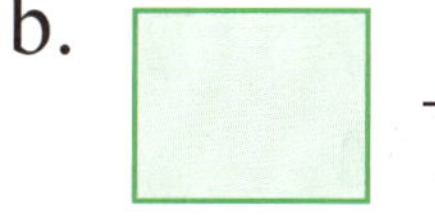 $= 3 + \frac{8}{10} =$ ____

$1 + 1 + 1 \quad \frac{8}{10}$

c. 

$1 + \frac{45}{100}$

$= 1 + \frac{45}{100} =$ ____

d. 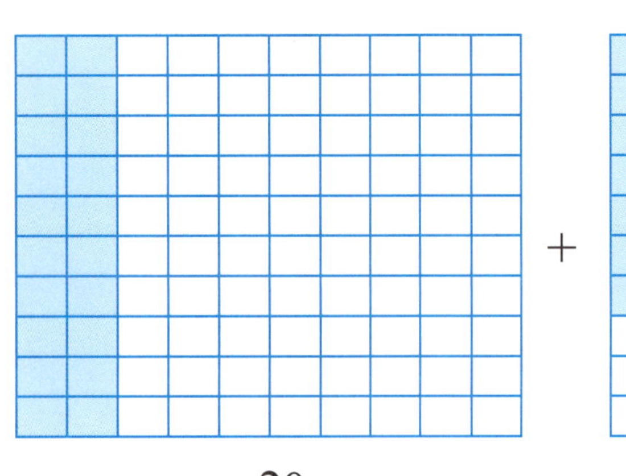

$\frac{20}{100} + \frac{7}{100}$

$= \frac{20}{100} + \frac{7}{100} =$ ______

2. Fill in the blanks

a. $2.45 = 2 + \frac{4}{10} +$ ______

b. $30.03 =$ ______ $+ \frac{\square}{100}$

c. $48.01 = 40 +$ ______ $+ \frac{\square}{100}$

d. $7.29 =$ ______ $+ \frac{\square}{10} + \frac{9}{\square}$

e. $2 + \frac{3}{10} + \frac{6}{100} =$ ______

f. $6 + \frac{2}{10} + \frac{5}{100} + \frac{8}{1000} =$ ______

g. $4 + \frac{6}{100} + \frac{1}{1000} =$ ______

h. $\frac{3}{10} + \frac{4}{1000} =$ ______

i. $\frac{1}{10} + \frac{1}{100} + \frac{1}{1000} =$ ______

j. $6 + \frac{2}{100} + \frac{0}{1000} =$ ______

Types of decimals

$\frac{4}{10}$

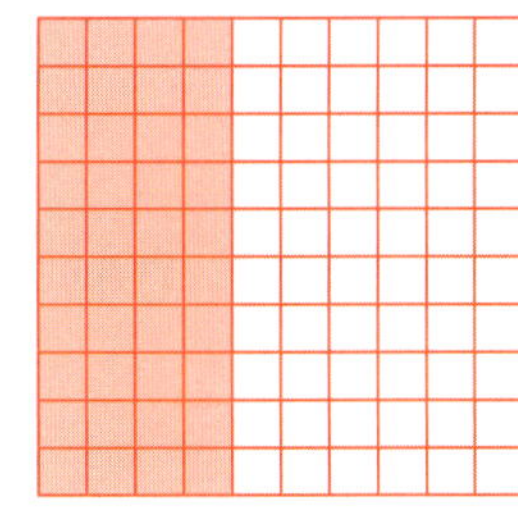

$\frac{40}{100}$

Total shaded portion is same in both squares.

Thus, $\frac{4}{10} = \frac{40}{100} = \frac{400}{1000}$

Which means 0.4 = 0.40 = 0.400

Decimals like 0.4, 0.40, 0.400 are equal in value and are called **equivalent decimals**.

So, we see writing or removing zeroes at the end of a decimal does not change its value.

EXAMPLE

Write equivalent decimals of 1.6; 2.45; 37.80

Solution : 1.6 = 1.60 = 1.600

2.45 = 2.450 = 2.4500

37.80 = 37.8 = 37.800

Like Decimals and Unlike Decimals

0.3; 3.8; 14.1; 6.4 are **like decimals**

4.24; 6.23; 12.26; 0.58 are also like decimals

Decimals which have same number of decimal places are called like decimals.

Decimals that have different number of decimal places are called **unlike decimals**.

0.8; 2.34; 6.003 are **unlike decimals**

0.4; 0.40; 0.400 are **unlike decimals**

Equivalent decimals can be unlike

Changing unlike decimals to like decimals

We see 1.8; 6.45; 14.507 are unlike decimals.

1.8 = 1.800 **Like decimals**

6.45 = 6.450 **Like decimals**

14.507 = 14.507 **Like decimals**

By adding zeroes, a group of unlike decimals can be changed to like decimals.

EXAMPLE

Change into like decimals

2.038; 1.5; 0.67

2.038 = 2.038
1.5 = 1.500
0.67 = 0.670

} **like decimals**

Comparison of decimals

To compare decimals, we should always have or take LIKE DECIMALS

EXAMPLE

Compare 6.4 and 6.48

Answer: 6.4 = 6.40

Now compare 6.40 and 6.48

Take whole numbers

So, 640 < 648

6.40 < 6.48

EXAMPLE

Compare 76.45 and 7.645

Answer: 76.45 = 76.450

7.645 = 7.645

76450 > 7645

76.450 > 7.645

Ordering of decimals

Students of class V went to the school clinic and recorded the weight of 4 students.

Anita = 35.5 kg

Sunita = 48 kg

Neha = 42.2 kg

Shreya = 40.8 kg

For comparison they were converted into like decimals.

35.5, 48.0, 42.2, 40.8

Ascending order

35.5, 40.8, 42.2, 48.0

Anita < Shreya < Neha < Sunita

 Exercise 5.3

1. Circle the smallest decimals

   a. 1.6, 1.74, 0.8, 0.29

   b. 0.71, 0.92, 0.81, 0.6

2. Fill in the box with >, < or =

a.	3.16		3.6	b.	12.1		12.01
c.	7.9		7.09	d.	0.62		0.260
e.	0.008		0.1	f.	6.35		6.419
g.	1.8		1.799	h.	0.98		0.9
i.	4.03		4.032	j.	0.2		1.19

3. Write in the ascending order using '<' symbol.

   a. 5.14; 6.041; 5.014; 5.41

   b. 3.71; 3.07; 3.87; 3.78

   c. 6.9; 5.09; 5.83; 5.38

   d. 19.03; 19.51; 9.35; 9.05

4. Write in descending order using the '>' symbol.

   a. 7.63; 70.063; 70.21; 7.6

   b. 10.05; 10.048; 10.023; 10.8

   c. 4.58; 5.3; 4.6; 5.03

   d. 49.4; 4.935; 49.35; 4.96

5. Write the 3 consecutive decimal numbers.

   a. 7.4; 7.5; 7.6; __________

   b. 1.16; 1.17; 1.18; __________

   c. 9.004; 9.005; 9.006; __________

   d. 17.86; 17.87; 17.88; __________

Addition and subtraction of decimals

EXAMPLE

Add 3.16 and 4.8

Solution:

```
    3. 1 6
  + 4. 8 0
  ---------
    7. 9 6
  ---------
```

Steps

- Convert into like decimals by adding zeroes.
- Place the decimal number one below the other as per place value system, means ones below ones, tenths below tenths and so on.
- Decimal point in same column.
- The decimals in the 'sum' (answer) is in the same column.

EXAMPLE

Add 12 and 6.83

Solution:

$$\begin{array}{r} 12.00 \\ +\ 6.83 \\ \hline 18.83 \\ \hline \end{array}$$

Add 5.67 + 3 + 2.589

Solution:

$$\begin{array}{r} 5.670 \\ +\ 3.000 \\ +\ 2.589 \\ \hline 11.259 \\ \hline \end{array}$$

Exercise 5.4

1. Add

   a. 0.3 + 3 + 33.36

   b. 23.71 + 2.536

   c. 525.05 + 33.6

   d. 10.48 + 16.6

   e. 1.9 + 21.84 + 7.6

   f. 16.391 + 2.51 + 1.8

   g. 40.06 + 65.5

   h. 0.04 + 5.39 + 2.718

2. Find the sum.

   a. 6 tenths + 14 hundredths + 28 thousandths

   b. 4 tenths + 37 thousandths + 8 tenths

   c. 3 ones 7 tenths + 4 hundreds + 4 thousands

Subtraction of decimals

Subtraction of decimals is similar to the subtraction of whole numbers.

EXAMPLE

22.6 from 38.97

Solution:

Steps

- Convert into like decimals if required.
- Write the smaller number below the greater number with the decimal (point) in the same column.
- Subtract (borrow if needed)
- Decimal in the answer should be in the same column as decimal of given numbers.

EXAMPLE

Subtract 27.83 from 52

Solution:

$$\begin{array}{r} 52.00 \\ -\ 27.83 \\ \hline 24.17 \\ \hline \end{array}$$

Exercise 5.5

1. Subtract

a. 7.31 – 6.08
b. 0.938 – 0.389
c. 31.01 – 30.11
d. 40.06 – 19.257
e. 11.821 – 6
f. 9.09 – 3.01
g. 4.53 – 3.35
h. 83.43 – 28.62
i. 20 – 19.638
j. 60 – 20.49

2. Subtract

a. 2.015 from 6
b. 29.09 from 42
c. 1.682 from 10
d. 5.992 from 7.07
e. 38.88 from 40.3
f. 3.88 from 11.1
g. 87.38 from 110.927
h. 41.8 from 60.404
i. 0.097 from 1
j. 0.003 from 0.03

Word Problems

Example : An empty box of sweet weighs 1.12 kg. Shiv puts 3.25 kg of sweets in the box. How much will the box weigh now?

Solution : Weight of empty box = 1.12 kg

Weight of sweets = 3.25 kg

Final weight of box = 4.37 kg

$$\begin{array}{r} 1.12 \\ +\ 3.25 \\ \hline 4.37 \\ \hline \end{array}$$

Example : A tank holds 40l of water. If 32.5l of water was used up, how much water is left in the tank?

Solution : Water in tank 40.0 l

Water used up 32.5 l

Water left 7.5 l

$$\begin{array}{r} {}^{3}4\ {}^{1\,9}0.\ {}^{1}0 \\ -\ 3\ 2.\ 5 \\ \hline 7.\ 5 \\ \hline \end{array}$$

Multiplication of decimals

Multiplication by a whole number

We know multiplication is repeated addition.

So, 3 times 0.3 is $0.3 + 0.3 + 0.3 = 0.9$

So, $3 \times 0.3 = 0.9$. 3 times 3 tenths is 9 tenths.

Let us see, 6 times $0.2 = 0.2 + 0.2 + 0.2 + 0.2 + 0.2 + 0.2 = 1.2$

$6 \times 0.2 = 1.2$

6 times 2 tenths = 12 tenths.

Thus, 7×0.8 = 7 times 8 tenths = 56 tenths = $\frac{56}{10} = 5.6$

3×0.14 = 3 tenths 14 hundredths = 42 hundredths = $\frac{42}{100} = 0.42$

We multiply a whole number with a decimal, just as we multiply whole numbers. In the product (answer) we put the decimals after as many digits from the right as in the multiplication.

1. So, 3.456×7

$$\begin{array}{r} 3.467 \\ \times\ 7 \\ \hline 24.269 \\ \hline \end{array}$$

2. 2.84×46

$$\begin{array}{r} 2.84 \\ \times\ 46 \\ \hline 1704 \\ +\ 11360 \\ \hline 130.64 \\ \hline \end{array}$$

3. 5×0.07

$$\begin{array}{r} 0.07 \\ \times\ 5 \\ \hline 0.35 \\ \hline \end{array}$$

Exercise 5.6

1. Multiply

a. 0.18×6 b. 0.03×8 c. 0.01×12 d. 0.23×9

e. 0.8×9 f. 0.52×7 g. 0.92×8 h. 4.37×46

i. 4×0.84 j. 7×0.79 k. 2.78×326 l. 6.31×81

m. 7.08×121 n. 5.006×65 o. 10.8×18 p. 0.004×37

q. 143.7×15 r. 3.71×21 s. 8.62×13 t. 1.06×20

2. Find the product and write in decimals also.

a. 5×6 tenths $=$ 30 tenths $= \frac{30}{10} = 3.0$

b. 8×7 hundredths $=$

c. 6×23 thousandths $=$

d. 9×14 tenths. $=$

e. 23×8 hundredths $=$

f. 14×4 thousandths $=$

3. Think and tell

a. A man filled 20 l of petrol in his car. The price of petrol per litre is ₹ 75, how much did he pay?

b. There are 4 cans of oil. Each can has 21.5 l of oil. Calculate the total amount of oil.

Multiplication by 10, 100, 1000 etc

Multiplying a decimal by 10, 100 or 1000 certainly results in a product which is greater (larger) than the given decimals.

$10 \times 13.7 = 137.0$

$10 \times 7.96 = 79.6$

$10 \times 0.481 = 4.81$

When a decimal is multiplied by 10, the decimal point moves to the right by one place, in the product.

$100 \times 6.81 = 681.0$

$100 \times 30.42 = 3042.0$

$100 \times 59.136 = 5913.6$

When a decimal is multiplied by 100, the decimal moves to the right by two places, in the product.

$1000 \times 0.0063 = 6.3$

$1000 \times 4.21 = 4210.0$

$1000 \times 81.5 = 8150.0$

When a decimal is multiplied by 1000, the decimal moves to the right by 3 places in the product.

Multiplication of a decimal by a decimal

EXAMPLE

Multiply 2.7 × 1.8

Solution: $2.7 \times 1.8 = \frac{27}{10} \text{x} \frac{18}{10}$

$= \frac{486}{100} = 4.86$

$2.7 \times 1.8 = 4.86$ (The product has 2 decimal places.)

EXAMPLE

Multiply 3.45 × 1.2

$$3.45 \times 1.2 = \frac{345}{100} \text{x} \frac{12}{10}$$

$$= 345 \text{x} \frac{12}{1000}$$

$$= \frac{4140}{1000}$$

$$= 4.140$$

3.45 × 1.2 = 4.140 The product has 3 decimal places which is the sum of the decimal places of 3.45 and 1.2

EXAMPLE

Multiply 4.15 × 3.8

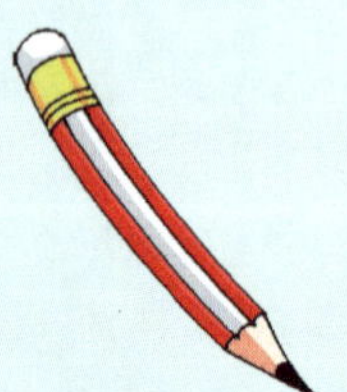

```
  4. 1 5
 × 3. 8
 -------

 -------
```

```
      4 1 5
    ×   3 8
  ---------
    3 3 2 0
  1 2 4 5 0
  ---------
  1 5 7 7 0
  ---------
```

Number of decimals places in 4.15 is 2 and 3.8 is 1. So, the number of decimal places in the product has to be 2 + 1 = 3.

- When two decimals are to be multiplied, we first multiply the whole numbers.
- Then the decimal point is placed in the product. The decimal place in the product is the sum of the places in the multiplier and the multiplicand.

Exercise 5.7

1. Find the product

a. 5.008×100 b. 23.06×100 c. 9.8×10

d. 611.005×100 e. 0.005×100 f. 77.1×100

g. 11.001×1000 h. 4.02×10 i. 157.2×10

j. 1.6×1000 k. 26.09×100 l. 0.03×1000

m. 0.79×1000 n. 0.908×100 o. 40.041×100

2. Find the product

a. 5.3×1.35 b. 33.03×4.4 c. 10.14×3.01

d. 88.08×1.5 e. 2.5×0.6 f. 1.47×2.9

g. 6.002×0.7 h. 79.09×3.21 i. 47.5×5.5

j. 0.14×0.6 k. 8.35×7.63 l. 0.225×0.15

m. 18.4×35.5 n. 0.07×0.4 o. 2.9×0.36

3. Fill in the blanks

1. 3.48×10 = ______
2. ______ $\times 10$ = 76.14
3. ______ $\times 10$ = 0.9
4. ______ $\times 100$ = 0.87
5. ______ $\times 100$ = 0.03
6. ______ $\times 1000$ = 162.5
7. ______ $\times 1000$ = 8532
8. ______ $\times 100$ = 2.7

4. If $15.8 \times 26.37 = 416.646$, find the value of

   a. 1.58×26.37

   b. 1.58×2.637

   c. 15.8×0.2637

   d. 0.158×0.2637

Word Problems

a. Cost of 1 kg of sugar is ₹ 31.50. Find the cost of 12 kg of sugar.

b. A car covers 45.2 km in one hour. Find the distance covered by the car in 7 hours.

c. A tin of oil weighs 10.25 kg. Find the weight of 16 such tins.

Division of decimals

EXAMPLE

Divide 15.6 kg by 3

$$= \frac{156}{10} \times \frac{1}{3}$$

$$= \frac{52}{10}$$

$$= 5.2$$

or

```
    5.2
 3)15.6(
   15
   ---
   x6
    6
   ---
    x
```

The decimals part in Quotient should be directly above the decimal point in the dividend.

EXAMPLE

Divide 0.24 by 4

$$= \frac{\cancel{24}^{\,6}}{100} \times \frac{1}{\cancel{4}_{\,1}}$$

$$= \frac{6}{100} = 0.06$$

or

```
      0.06
  4 ) 0.24 (
      0.
      ----
       2
      -00
      ----
       24
      -24
      ----
        x
      ----
```

EXAMPLE

Divide 24.60 ÷ 4

$$= \frac{\cancel{2460}^{\,615}}{100} \times \frac{1}{\cancel{4}_{\,1}}$$

$$= 6.15$$

or

```
       6.15
  4 ) 24.60 (
     - 24
     -----
       x 6
       - 4
       ---
        20
      - 20
      ----
         x
      ----
```

Note: Decimal point is put only in the dividend and the quotient and nowhere else in the steps of division.

Exercise 5.8

1. Divide

a. $\frac{9.6}{4}$ e. $\frac{12.8}{8}$ i. $\frac{6.25}{5}$ m. $\frac{40.5}{5}$

b. $\frac{30.3}{3}$ f. $\frac{52.4}{4}$ j. $\frac{3.05}{5}$ n. $\frac{49.7}{7}$

c. $\frac{1.26}{6}$ g. $\frac{83.93}{11}$ k. $\frac{48.8}{8}$ o. $\frac{28.7}{7}$

d. $\frac{0.45}{9}$ h. $\frac{0.48}{6}$ l. $\frac{0.81}{9}$

Division when divisor is greater than divided

Divide 4.256 by 8

$$
\begin{array}{r}
0.532 \\
8\overline{)\,4.256} \\
-\,40 \\
\hline
25 \\
-\,24 \\
\hline
016 \\
-\,16 \\
\hline
0
\end{array}
$$

Answer 0.532

Since 4 < 8, we put 0 in the ones place in the quotient and put a decimal point after that corresponding to the decimal point in the dividend.

EXAMPLE

Divide 5.859 by 9

```
     0.651
 9 ) 5.859
   - 54
     45
   - 45
     009
   -   9
       0
```

Answer 0.651

Divide 0.372 by 12

```
     0.031
 9 ) 0.372
   - 36
      12
   -  12
      00
```

Answer 0.031

We put 0 to follow by a decimal in the quotient. Now 3 < 12 Hence a 'o' is put is the tenth place. We take 37 and proceed.

Study this division carefully.

EXAMPLE

Divide 36.9 by 15

```
      2.46
 15 ) 36.90   ←—— Add a zero here
    - 30
       69
    -  60
       90
    -  90
        0
```

Divide 53.9 ÷ 4

```
     13.475
 4 ) 53.900
   - 4
     13
   - 12
      19
    - 16
       30
     - 28
        20
      - 20
         0
```

So, we see we can add as many zeroes as we need in the dividend after the decimal in order to get a remainder 0.

Exercise 5.9

1. Divide

a. $2.36 \div 4$
b. $0.48 \div 12$
c. $0.424 \div 8$
d. $1.68 \div 7$
e. $0.153 \div 3$
f. $7.68 \div 6$
g. $5.2 \div 13$
h. $2.48 \div 8$
i. $9.45 \div 3$
j. $3.12 \div 15$
k. $10.78 \div 7$
l. $0.77 \div 11$
m. $140.58 \div 100$
n. $67.8 \div 8$
o. $202.4 \div 16$
p. $5.6 \div 8$
q. $350.52 \div 23$
r. $424.25 \div 25$
s. $37.86 \div 12$
t. $83.4 \div 8$
u. $53.9 \div 4$

Division by 10, 100, 1000 etc

$$7 \div 10 = \frac{7}{10} = 0.7$$

$$3.5 \div 10 = \frac{35}{10} \text{ x } \frac{1}{10} = \frac{35}{100} = 0.35$$

$$6.85 \div 10 = \frac{685}{100} \text{ x } \frac{1}{10} = \frac{685}{1000} = 0.685$$

$$45.38 \div 100 = \frac{45.38}{100} \text{ x } \frac{1}{10} = \frac{4538}{10000} = 0.4538$$

$$8.72 \div 1000 = \frac{872}{100} \text{ x } \frac{1}{1000} = \frac{872}{100000} = 0.00872$$

Thus we see,

* When we divide by 10, then decimal point is shifted to the left by one place.
* When divided by 100, then decimal point is shifted to the left by two places.
* When divided by 1000, the decimal point shifts to the left by 3 places.

EXAMPLE

Division by 10, 100, 1000 etc

$$8.48 \div 20 = \frac{8.48}{10} \times \frac{1}{2}$$

$$= \frac{0.848}{2}$$

$$= 0.424$$

Divide first by 10 and then by 2

EXAMPLE

$$\frac{46.5}{500} = \frac{46.5}{100} \times \frac{1}{5}$$

$$= \frac{0.465}{5}$$ (Divide first by 100 then by 5)

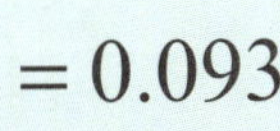

$$= 0.093$$

Exercise 5.10

1. Divide

a. $243.2 \div 10$	b. $28.3 \div 100$	c. $6.75 \div 100$
d. $0.2 \div 10$	e. $2.36 \div 100$	f. $0.1 \div 10$
g. $75.65 \div 1000$	h. $0.6 \div 100$	i. $126.4 \div 100$
j. $19.27 \div 1000$	k. $2.8 \div 100$	l. $7.348 \div 100$
m. $42.9 \div 10$	n. $16 \div 100$	o. $265 \div 1000$

2. Divide

a. $383.14 \div 20$	b. $37.26 \div 600$	c. $50.4 \div 70$
d. $489.3 \div 3000$	e. $73.92 \div 6000$	f. $8.469 \div 90$
g. $5.36 \div 400$	h. $41.2 \div 80$	i. $51.31 \div 70$

3. Fill in the blanks

a. $628.4 \div$ _____ $= 62.84$	b. $2 \div$ _____ $= 0.002$
c. $59.2 \div$ _____ $= 0.592$	d. $176.9 \div$ _____ $= 0.01769$
e. $17.4 \div$ _____ $= 0.0174$	f. $0.8 \div$ _____ $= 0.08$
h. $4.01 \div$ _____ $= 0.0401$	g. $33 \div$ _____ $= 3.3$

More about Decimals

Division of a whole number or a decimal by a decimal

Do you remember, in order to find equivalent fractions of say $\frac{1}{4}$ what did we do?

$$\frac{1}{4} = \frac{1x5}{4x5} = \frac{5}{20} = \frac{1}{4}$$

$$\frac{1}{4} = \frac{1x10}{4x10} = \frac{10}{40} = \frac{1}{4}$$

That is in a fraction the numerator and the denominator can be **multiplied** by the **same number**.

Thus,

1. $8 \div 0.2 = \frac{8}{0.2} = \frac{8x10}{0.2x10} = \frac{80}{2} = 40$

2. $24.4 \div 0.04 = \frac{28.8x100}{0.04x100} = \frac{2880}{4} = 720$

3. $52.92 \div 1.2 = \frac{52.92x10}{1.2x10} = \frac{50}{125} = 0.4$

So, when the divisor is a decimal number:

* Convert the divisor into a whole number by multiplying with 10, 100 or 1000.
* Multiply the numerator with the same number (10, 100 or 1000)
* Divide the new dividend by the whole number divisor.

Exercise 5.11

1. Divide

a. 20.4 ÷ 0.04	b. 48.8 ÷ 0.8	c. 27.9 ÷ 0.9
d. 0.7515 ÷ 0.06	e. 89.64 ÷ 1.2	f. 3.85 ÷ 0.05
g. 18.6 ÷ 0.06	h. 5.55 ÷ 1.5	i. 350.52 ÷ 0.23
j. 0.9 ÷ 0.03	k. 4.8 ÷ 0.24	l. 3.12 ÷ 0.04

Division of a whole number by a whole number

Divide 5 by 4

$$5 \div 4 = \frac{5}{4} = \frac{5.0}{4}$$

$$\begin{array}{r} 1.25 \\ 4\overline{)5.00} \\ \underline{4} \\ 10 \\ \underline{8} \\ 20 \\ \underline{20} \\ 0 \end{array}$$

← Add zeros after decimal as many as we need till a remainder 0 is obtained.

Answer 1.25

EXAMPLE

Divide 6 by 15

$$\begin{array}{r} 0.4 \\ 15\overline{)6.4} \\ \underline{60} \\ 0 \end{array}$$

Answer 0.4

EXAMPLE

Divide 7 by 21

$$\begin{array}{r} 0.333 \\ 21\overline{)7.00} \\ \underline{6.3} \\ 70 \\ \underline{63} \\ 70 \\ \underline{63} \\ 7 \end{array}$$

Here we get 3 in the quotient repeatedly. So we stop dividing after 3 places of decimal and leave the quotient at that.

This method helps us to convert fractions into decimals.

Exercise 5.12

1. Convert the following fraction into decimals.

a. $\frac{3}{4}$	b. $\frac{1}{8}$	c. $\frac{5}{8}$	d. $\frac{1}{4}$
e. $\frac{3}{5}$	f. $\frac{1}{10}$	g. $2\frac{1}{5}$	h. $7\frac{1}{2}$
i. $5\frac{7}{9}$	j. $5\frac{1}{6}$	k. $6\frac{1}{4}$	l. $7 \div 12$

2. 93.45 kg of rice is packed in 15 bags. How much rice does each bag contain?

3. $3\frac{1}{2}$ tickets cost ₹ 367.50. What is the cost of 1 ticket?

4. A 6 m long ribbon was cut into 8 equal pieces. What was the length of each piece?

5. The weight of 100 drums of oil is ₹ 175.8 kg what will be the weight of 1 such drum?

6. ₹ 233.75 was distributed among some people. If each person got ₹ 13.75 how many people were present?

7. Product of 2 number is 0.0184. If one number is 0.8, find the other number.

8. 15.45 kg of biscuits is emptied into 5 boxes. Then each box of biscuits is packed into 3 tins. Find the weight of biscuits in each tin.

Estimation or Rounding Off

We have already done estimation (rounding) of whole numbers. The same rules apply for decimals as well.

Let us study some examples:

Round off to the nearest one

3.4 ⟶ since it is closer to 3 we round it off to 3 ones.

4.7 ⟶ It is closer to 5, so it is rounded to 5 ones

17.5 ⟶ round off to 18

So, in order to round to ones place we have to look at the digit in the next place, that is the tenths place.

Rounding to tenths place

1.87 ⟶ 1.9

5.42 ⟶ 5.4

19.19 ⟶ 19.2

216.04 ⟶ 216.0

0.08 ⟶ 0.1

Rounding hundredths to ones

8.68 ⟶ 9 ones

17.15 ⟶ 17 ones

214.97 ⟶ 215 ones

Rounding the decimal up to hundredths place or 2 decimals places

12.6937 ⟶ 12.69

6.039 ⟶ 6.04

0.099 ⟶ 0.10

11.565 ⟶ 11.57

2.008 ⟶ 2.01

So, if a number has to be rounded off to the hundredths place, the digit in the hundredths place is increased by 1, If the digit in the thousandths the place is 5, 6, 7, 8, 9. The digit in the hundredths place remains the same if the digit in the thousandths place is 0, 1, 2, 3 or 4.

Exercise 5.13

1. Round the decimal to the nearest ones place.

   a. 7.39 b. 12.07 c. 7.7 d. 20.5

   e. 141.5 f. 0.84 g. 0.48 h. 19.8

2. Round to the nearest tenth

   a. 64.92 b. 5.79 c. 10.95 d. 130.72

   e. 16.319 f. 227.23 g. 28.46 h. 44.44

3. Round to the nearest hundredths place

   a. 7.328 b. 0.275 c. 1.333 d. 9.999

   e. 0.666 f. 4.009 g. 0.059 h. 0.043

4. Express the following fraction correct up to two decimal places.

   a. $\frac{1}{8}$ b. $\frac{4}{3}$ c. $\frac{2}{11}$ d. $\frac{7}{15}$

Mental Maths

1. Express as decimals

   a. Seventeen thousandths

   b. Six and six tenths

   c. Two hundreds and two hundredths

   d. $900 + 9 + \frac{9}{1000}$

   e. $2000 + 40 + 6 + \frac{7}{10} + \frac{8}{1000}$

2. Choose the correct answers to fill in the blanks

   a. 0.065 ______ 0.65 (>, <, =)

   b. 8.02 and 9.73 are ________ decimals (like, unlike)

   c. 0.100 _______ 0.1 (>, <, =)

   d. 50.379 in expanded form is ___________________

   e. 0.4 of a metre = ________ cm = ________ mm.

6 Simplification of Numerical Expressions

Till now we have performed the four basic operations in Maths like addition, subtraction, multiplication and division. But we performed only one operation at a time.

Let us learn to simplify numerical expressions with two or more operations.

Say for example,

$20 + 16 \div 4 \times 3 - 4$

Let us simplify this by various methods

First method

$= (20 + 16 \div 4) \times 3 - 4$

$= (36 \div 4) \times 3 - 4$

$= 9 \times 3 - 4$

$= 27 - 4$

$= 23$

Answer: 23

Second method

$= (20 + 16) \div (4 \times 3) - 4$

$= 36 \div (12 - 4)$

$= 36 \div 8$

$= 4.5$

Answer: 4.5

Third method

$= 20 + (16 \div 4) \times 3 - 4$

$= (20 + 4) \times 3 - 4$

$= 24 \times 3 - 4$

$= 72 - 4$

$= 68$

Answer: 68

Fourth method

$= 20 + (16 \div 4) \times 3 - 4$

$= 20 + (4 \times 3) - 4$

$= 20 + 12 - 4$

$= 32 - 4$

$= 28$

Answer: 28

There are more ways in which this can be solved. What we observe is that a simplifying the numerical expression in four different ways gave us 4 different answers. Obviously all of them cannot be correct. How can we get the correct solution?

To obtain the correct answer (or solution) we should follow a particular order in which the operations are to be performed.

It is BODMAS.	**ORDER**
B - Brackets	– Solve with in brackets
O - of	– Next 'of'
D - Division	– Division
M - Multiplication	– Then 'X'
A - Addition S - Subtraction	– whichever comes first

* There are 3 kinds of brackets

[ ] Square	– last solved
{ } Curly	– Second to be solved
( ) Curved	– First to be solved.

Thus, fourth method is the correct method.

EXAMPLE

$= 50 - [20 - \{11 + (7 - 3 \times 2)\}]$

$= 50 - [20 - \{11 + (7 - 6)\}]$

$= 50 - [20 - \{11 + 1\}]$

$= 50 - [20 - 12]$

$= 50 - 8 = 42$ Ans.

Exercise 6.1

1. Simplify

a. $18 + 16 \div 2$

b. $24 - 18 \div 6$

c. $28 \div 7 - 3$

d. $48 \div 8 + 4$

e. $\frac{3}{5} x \frac{5}{9} - \frac{1}{5}$

f. $4.2 \div 0.6 - 2.5 \div 5$

g. $7.2 - 0.4 \times 0.3$

h. $0.35 \times 100 + 0.4 \times 10$

i. $2 \times 0.3 + 0.5 \times 0.7$

j. $\frac{4}{7} - \frac{1}{7} x \frac{14}{9}$

k. $5\frac{1}{5} \div \frac{13}{10} + \frac{1}{4}$

l. $\frac{3}{8} \div \frac{1}{24} x \frac{1}{6}$

2. Simplify and solve

a. $(4 \times 8) + 9$

b. $4 \times (8 + 9)$

c. $4 \times (5 - 2)$

d. $(4 \times 5) - 2$

e. $3.5 \times (1.41 + 2.34)$

f. $100 - [88 - \{56 + (32 - 16)\}]$

g. $\frac{1}{2} \div \left\{2\frac{1}{4} - \left(\frac{1}{3} + \frac{1}{2}\right)\right\}$

h. $\frac{1}{2} \div \left\{2\frac{1}{4} - \left(\frac{1}{3} + \frac{1}{2}\right)\right\}$

i. $3\,[19 \div \{1 + 8\,(13 - 6)\}]$

j. $2\,[15.2 + \{4.5 + 11.5\} \times 2]$

3. Simplify the following

a. $7 - \{5.54 - (4.3 - 1.49)\}$

b. $1\frac{1}{6} + \left\{5\frac{1}{3} + \left(\frac{21}{66} \div \frac{7}{11}\right)\right\}$

c. $78 \div 6 + 5 \times 6 - 40$

d. $19 + 51 \div 17 - 28 + 29$

e. $8 + 6 \div 2 \times 7 + 60 \div 6$

f. $[100 - \{90 - (20 \times 3) \div 2]$

7 Geometry

Lines, Rays and Line Segments

A line segment has two ends points

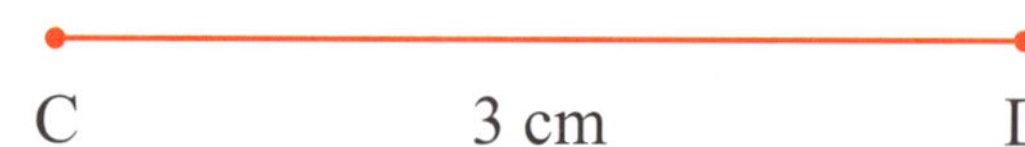

$\overleftrightarrow{CD}$ is a line segment of length 3cm. We can read it as $\overleftrightarrow{DC}$ also.

A line extends end lessly on both sides.

A line can only be represented on a sheet of paper or any plane.

$\overleftrightarrow{XY}$ is a line (or can be read as y x also)

A ray is a part of a line and etends endlessly in one direction only.

$\overleftrightarrow{AB}$ is a ray.

Intersecting Lines

When two lines or line segments cross or cut each other, they are called **intersecting lines** or intersecting segments. The point where they cross or cut each other is called the **point of intersection**.

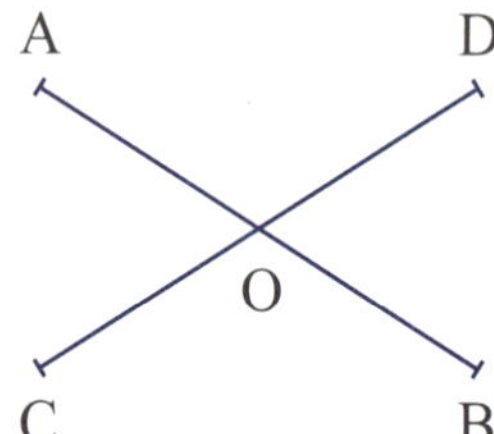

$\overleftrightarrow{AB}$ and $\overleftrightarrow{CD}$ are **intersecting lines** and O is the **point of intersection**.

Parallel Lines

Lines that never meet are called **parallel lines**. They are at an equal distance from each other.

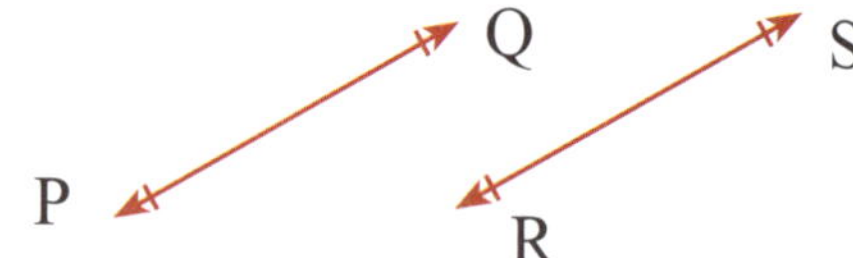

XYLLWZ

$\overleftrightarrow{PQ}$ and $\overleftrightarrow{RS}$ are parallel to each other.

The geometrical symbol for parallel lines is II

Perpendicular Lines

They are intersecting lines, but have a special property, that they cut or cross at right angles.

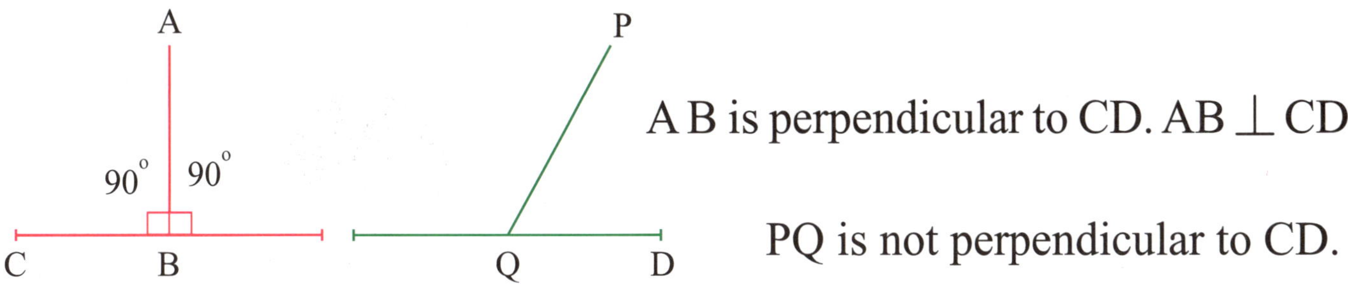

A B is perpendicular to CD. AB ⊥ CD

PQ is not perpendicular to CD.

Exercise 7.1

1. Name the line or lines given below.

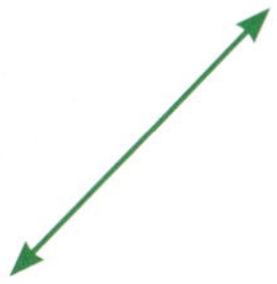

_______   _______, _______   _______, _______   _______, _______

_______, _______, _______   _______, _______   _______, _______

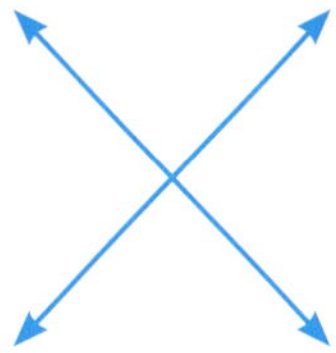

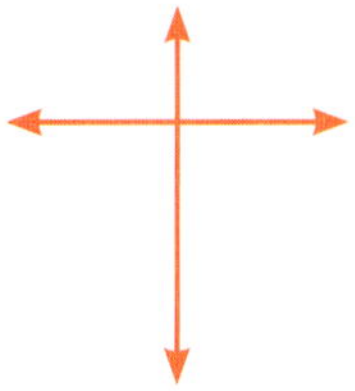

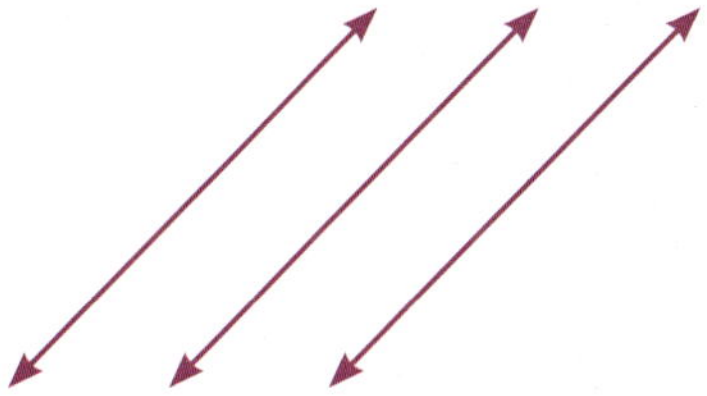

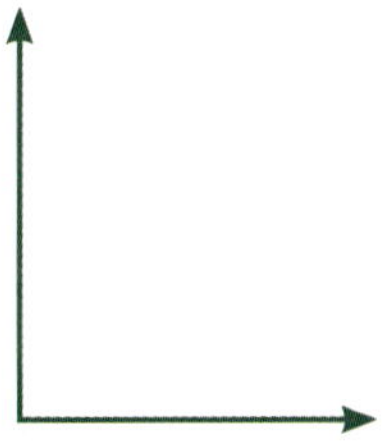

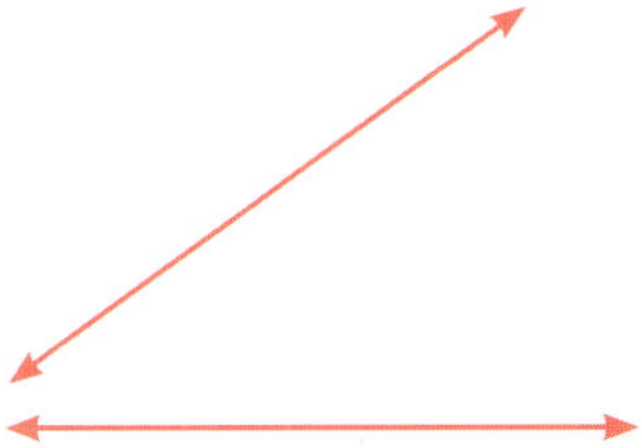

Parallel lines	Intersecting lines	Perpendicular lines

Angles

When two rays meet at a point an angle is formed.

The point at which the rays meet is called vertex of the angle.

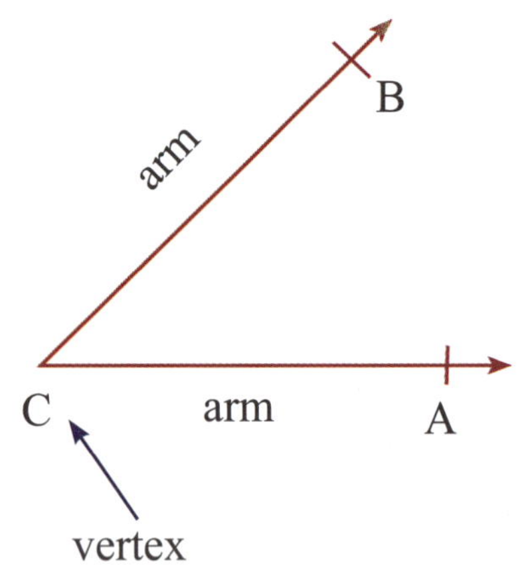

Naming an angle

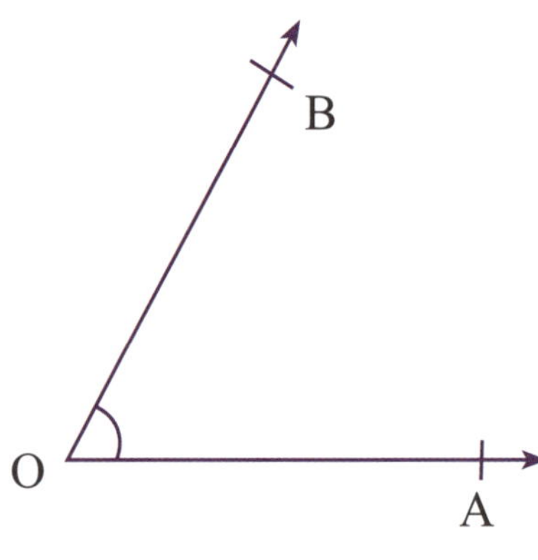

Ray $\overleftrightarrow{OB}$ and $\overleftrightarrow{OA}$ make $\angle BOA$

While naming an angle the vertex has to be in the middle.

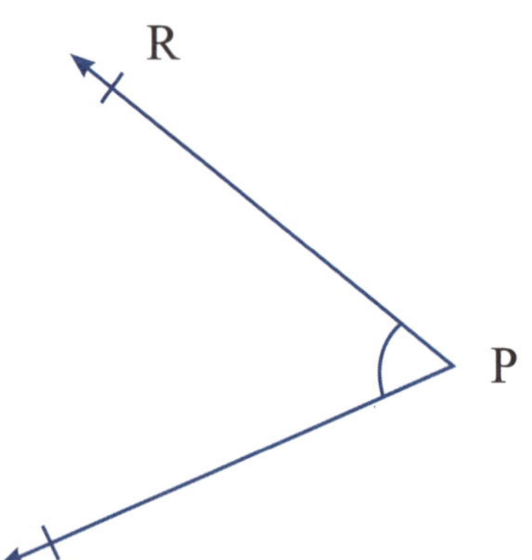

This is $\angle RPQ$ or $\angle QPR$

Interior and exterior of angles

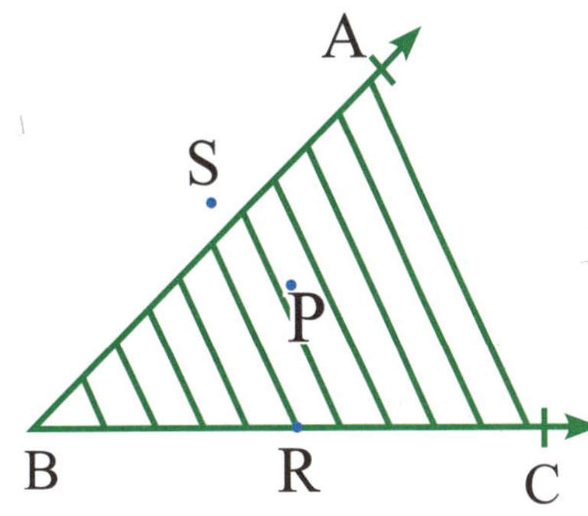

The shaded portion is the interior of the angle ABC.

P is in the **interior** of ∠ABC

S lies in the **exterior** of ∠ABC

R lies on the angle ∠ABC

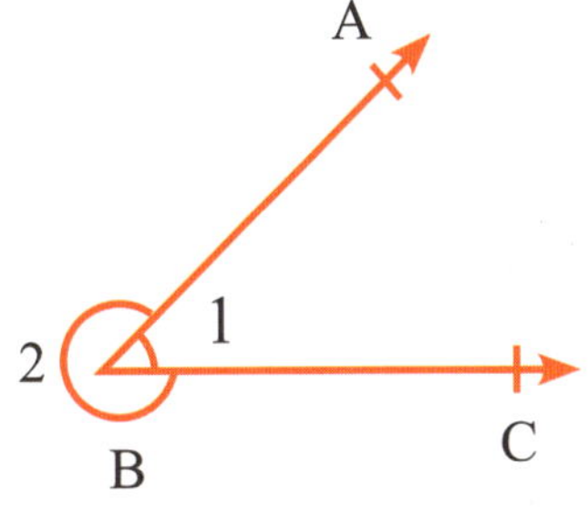

∠1 is an interior angle

∠2 is an exterior angle

Exercise 7.2

1. Which of the following figures are angles?

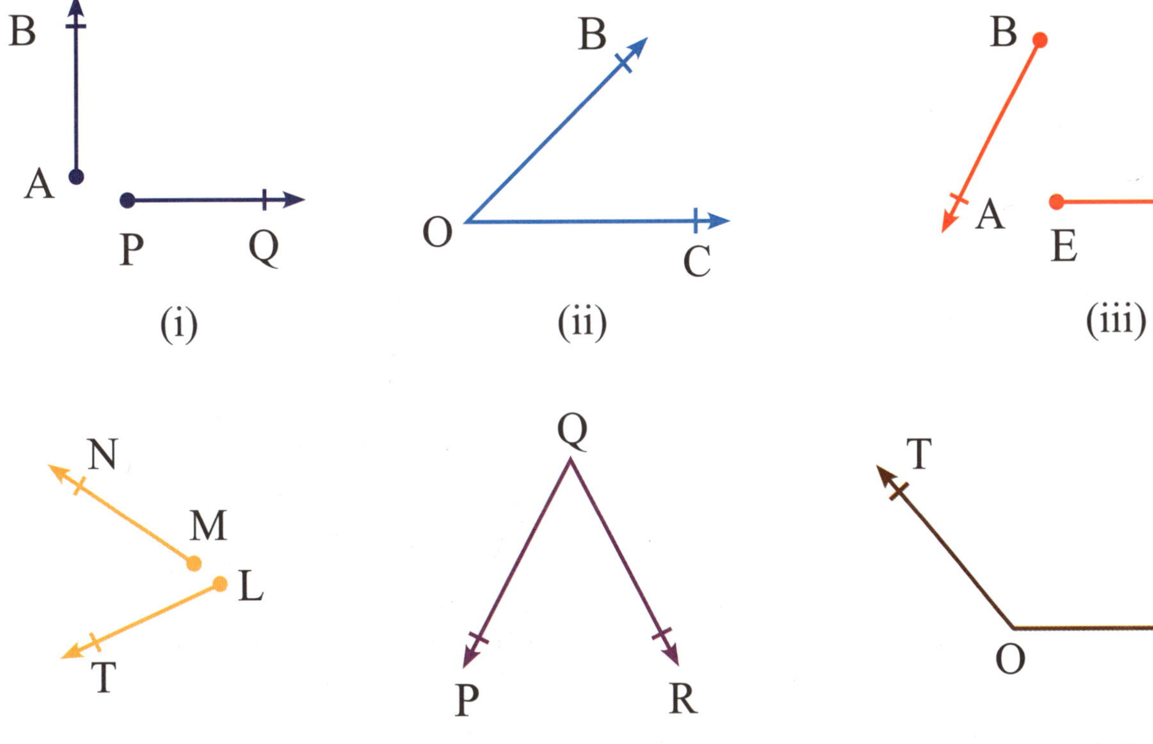

2. Name each angle.

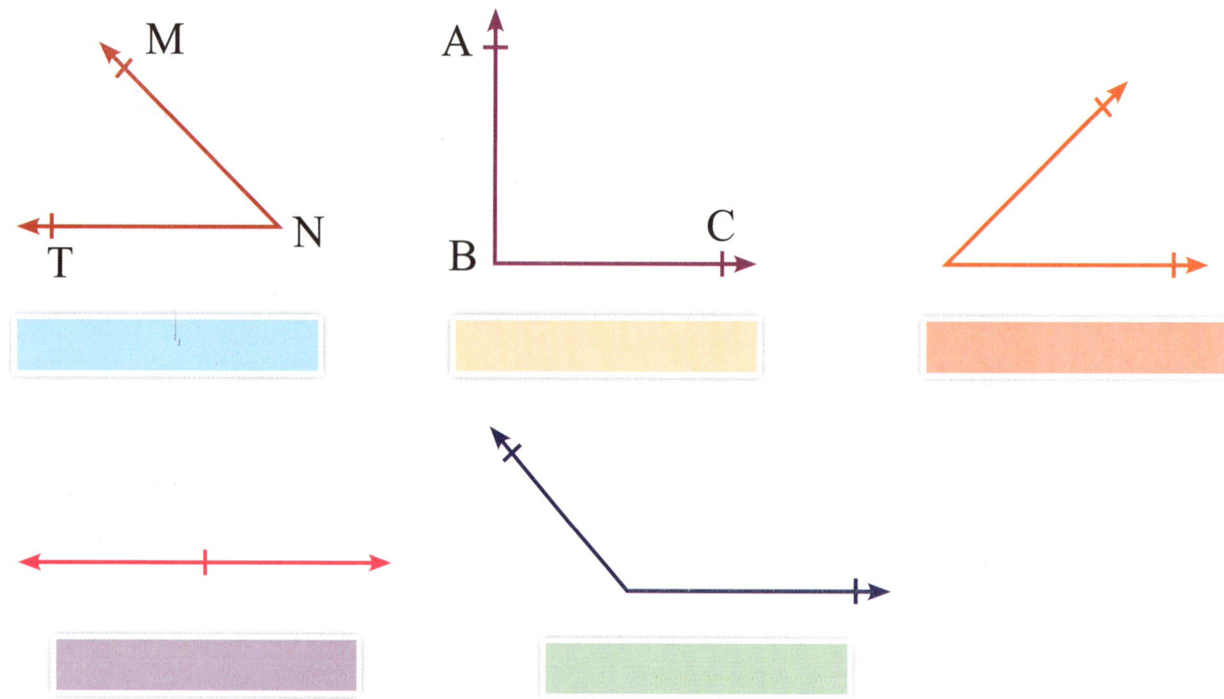

3. Name all possible angles formed in each figure.

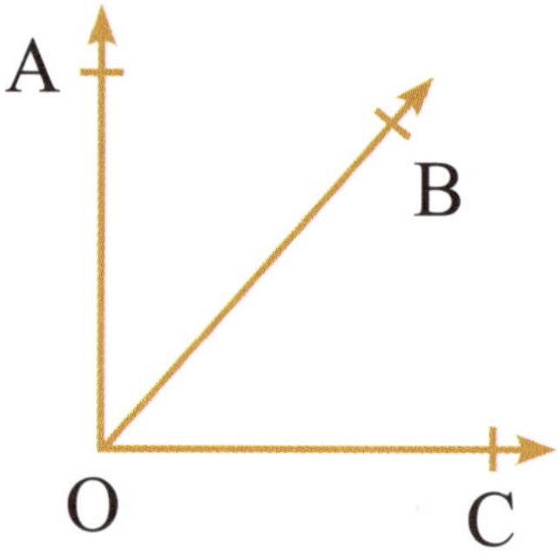

A B O C

(i)

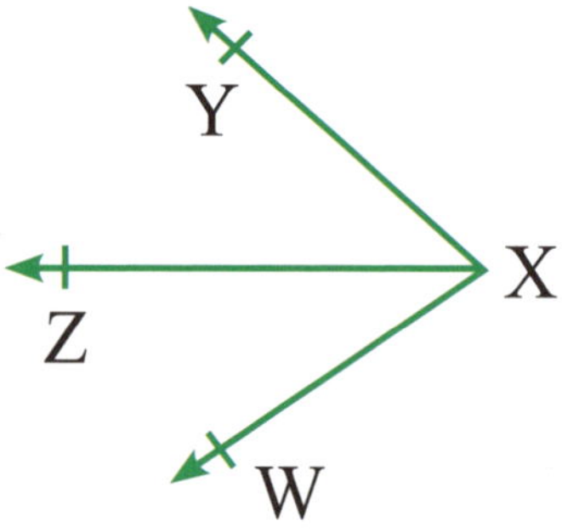

Y X Z W

(ii)

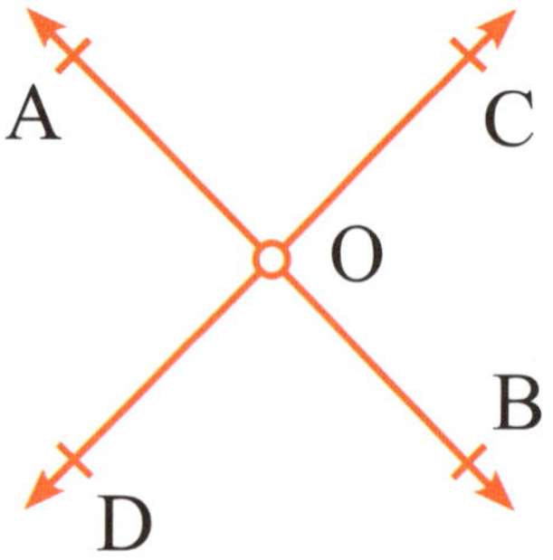

A C O B D

(iii)

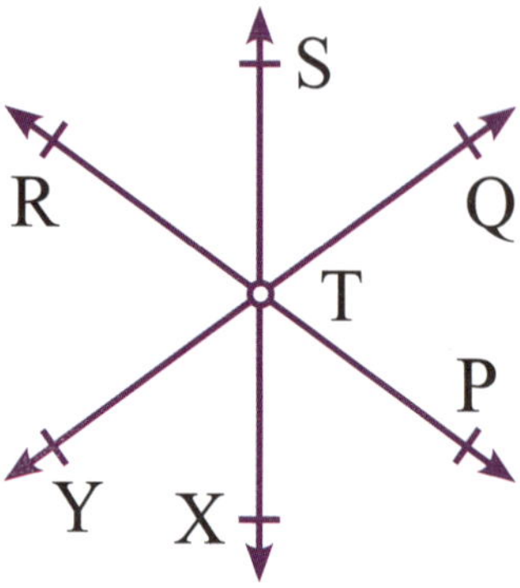

S R Q T P Y X

(iv)

Measuring angles

To measure an angle, a **protractor** is used. It can be found in an **instrument** (geometry) box.

Look at the protractor carefully.

It has two scales.

A
Base line
C
centre

One on the inside called **inner**

scale and the other on the outside called the **outer scale**.

The inner and outer scale has numbers from 0 to 180.

An angle is measured in degrees.

A protractor can read from right to left or left to right.

Consider ∠ABC

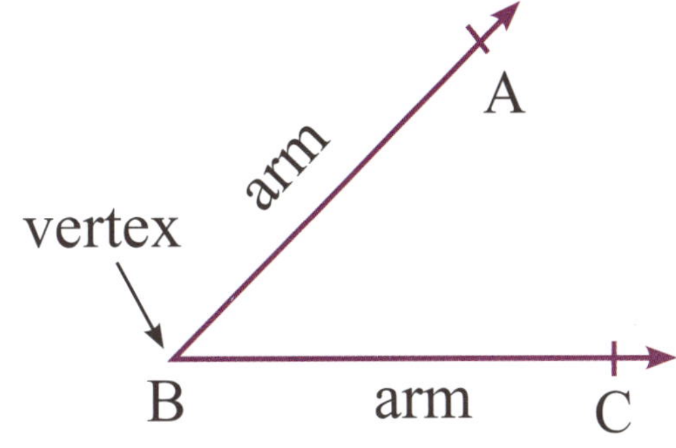

- Place the protractor such that on vertex B, the centre of protractor is placed. The base line of protractor is on arm BC
- Read the angle where BA cuts the scale of the protractor. Here BA cuts at 50°.

We write m ∠ABC = 50° (measure of ∠ABC = 50 degree)

Consider ∠XYZ

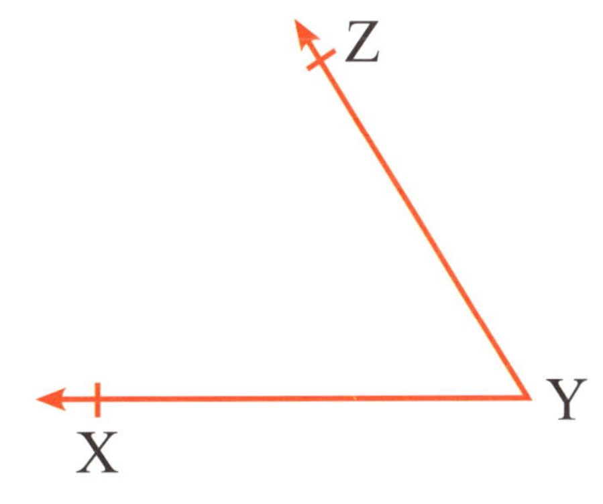

We measure ∠XYZ like this.

m ∠xyz=

Since YX is facing left, it is measured on the outer scale.

Consider ∠PQR

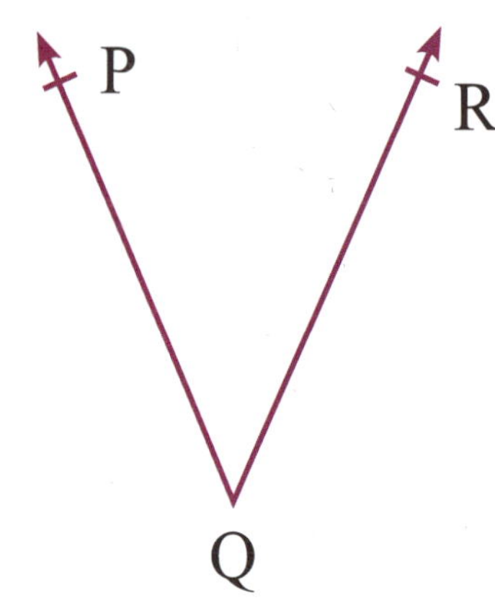

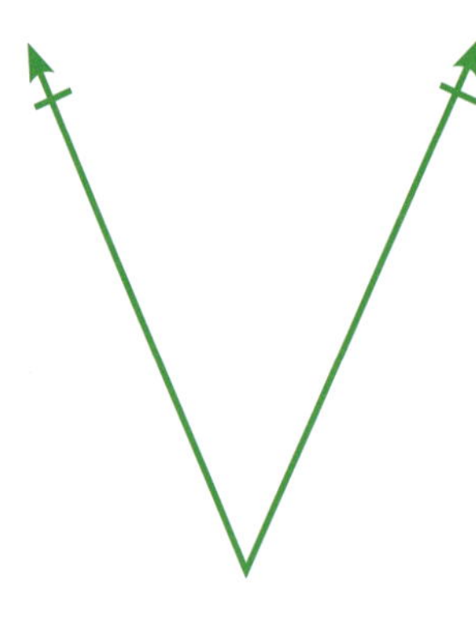

∠PQR =

Always measure from 0° to 180°

 Exercise 7.3

1. Measure the following angles using a protractor

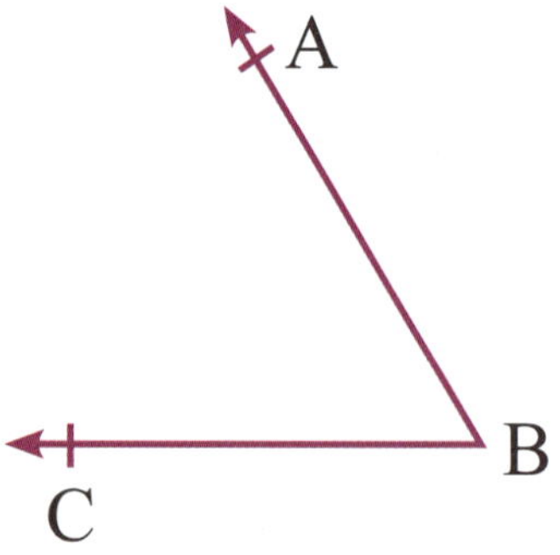

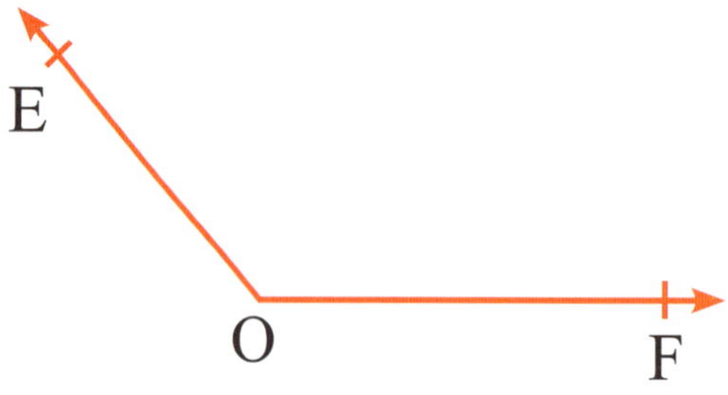

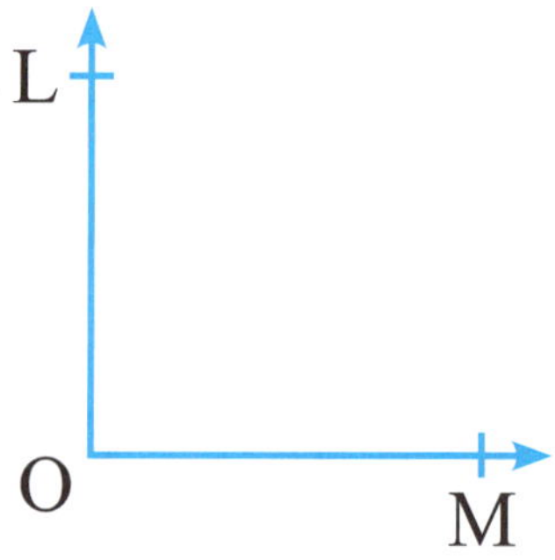

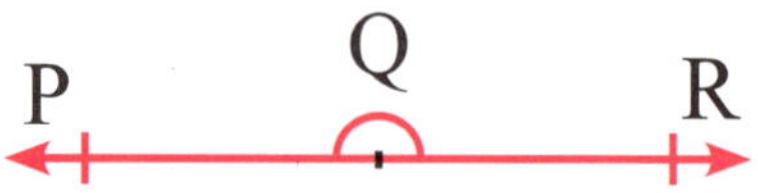

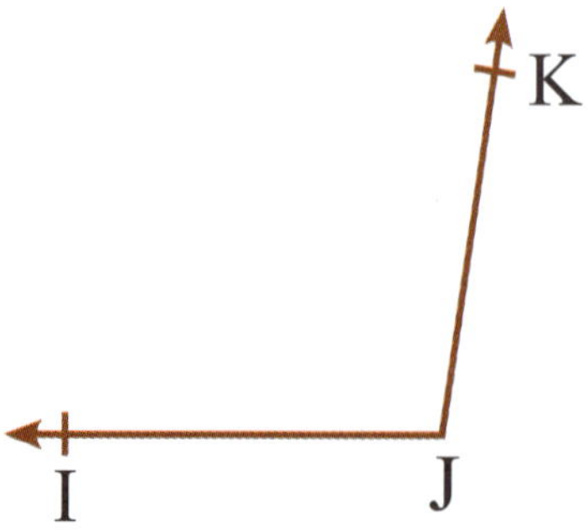

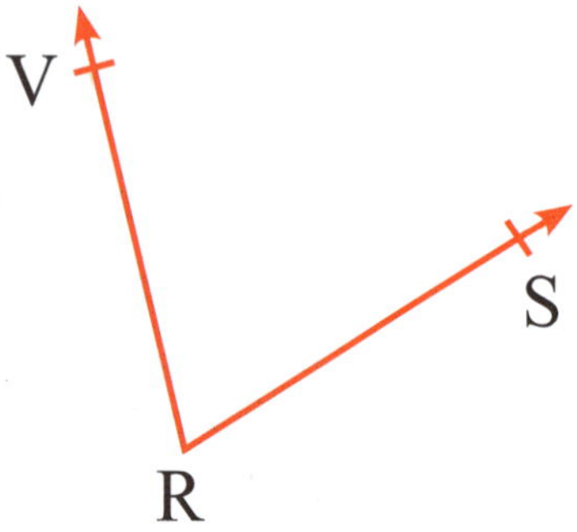

Draw angles of a given measurement.

Draw an angle of 110 degree.

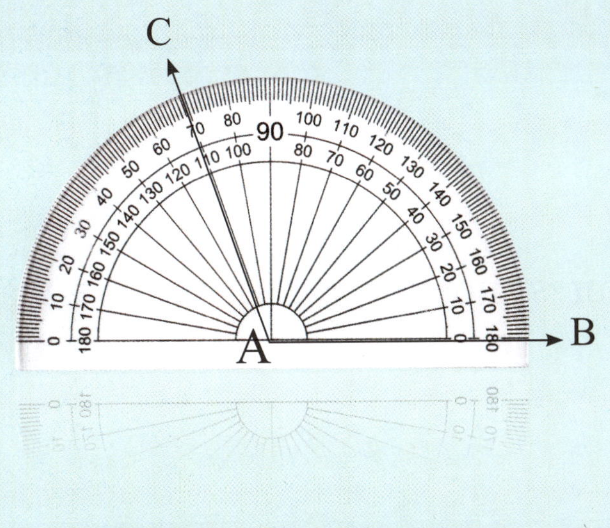

Follow these steps:

1. Draw AB horizontally.
2. Place protractor on AB with centre of protractor on A.
3. Start from 0 degree or ray AB till 110 degree (on inner scale) and put a point C against 110°.
4. Remove protractor and draw a straight line from vertex A through C.

$\angle CAB = 110°$

Exercise 7.4

1. Use a protractor and a ruler to draw these angles.

a. 30°	b. 40°	c. 70°	d. 90°	e. 110°
f. 120°	g. 140°	h. 45°	i. 125°	j 105°

Types of angles

Acute angle: An angle which measures between 0 ° to 90°

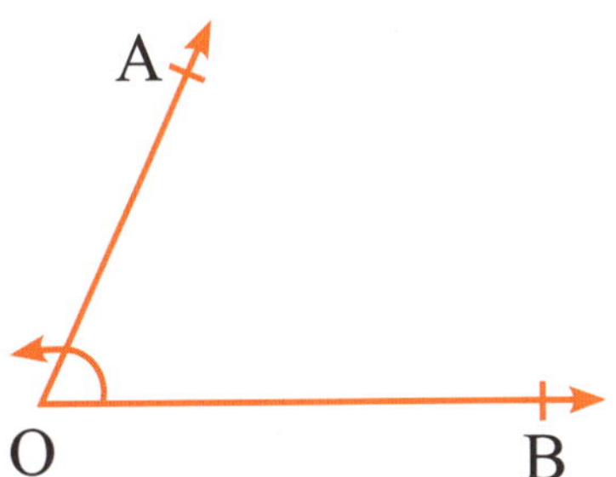

Right angle: An angle which measures 90°

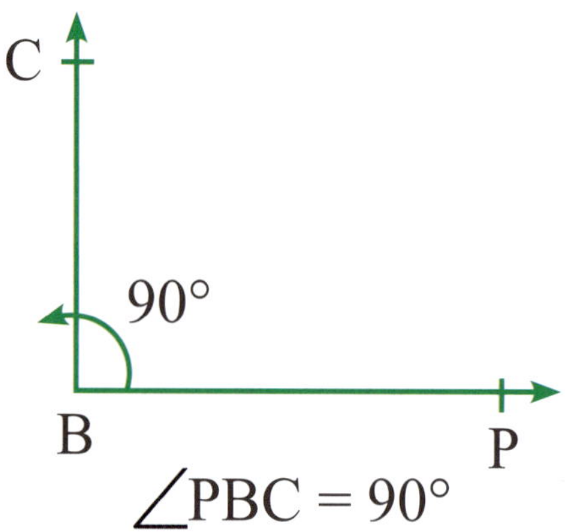

∠PBC = 90°

Obtuse angle: An angle which measures more than 90° but less than 180°

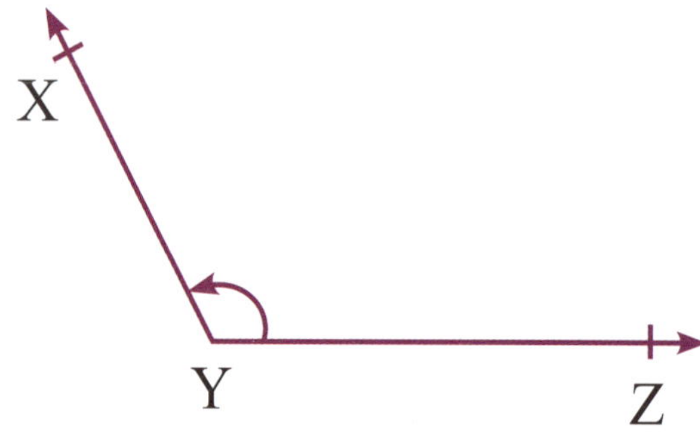

Straight angle: An angle measuring 180 °

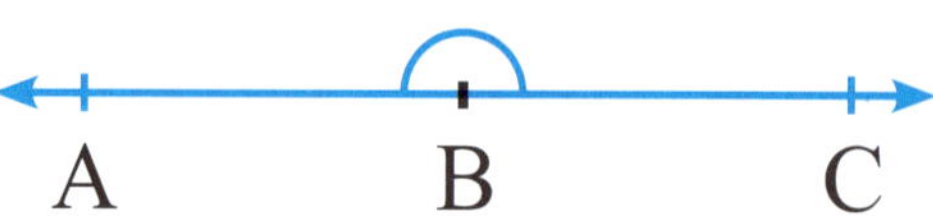

Zero angle: An angle measuring 0 °

Collinear points

Three or more points which lie on the same line are called collinear points.

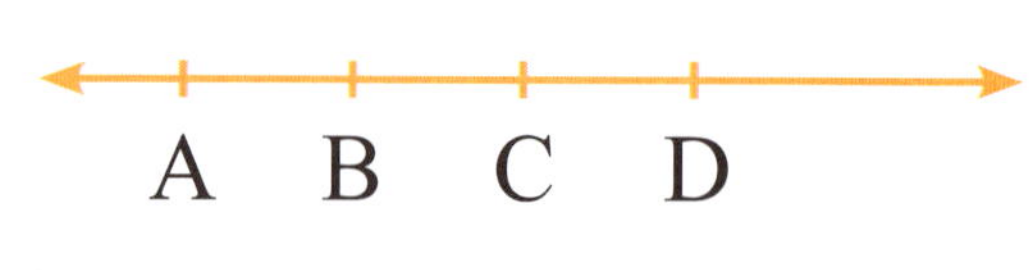

A, B, C, D, are called collinear

Non-collinear points

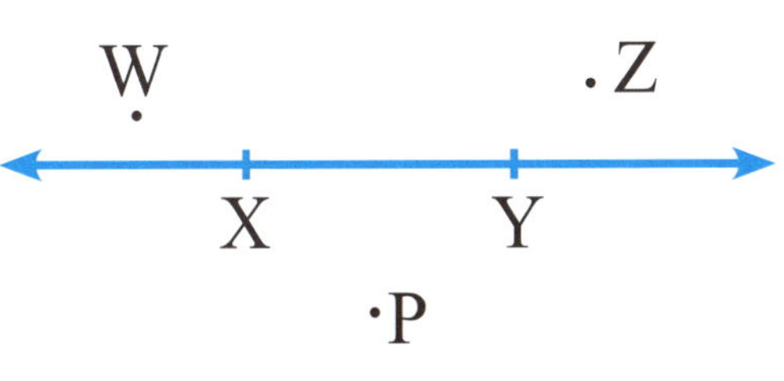

When three or more points do not lie on the same line, these points are called non-collinear.

Triangles

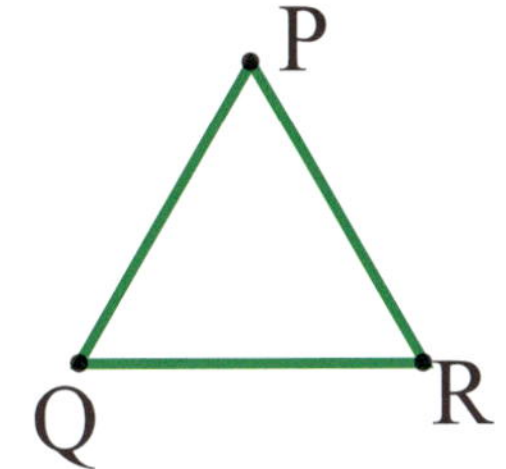

Look at the three non collinear points P, Q, R

Join P to Q, Q to R and R to P.

What do we get? We get a triangle PQR. So, when three non collinear points are joined (taking 2 at a time) we get a triangle.

A triangle is a closed figure made up of three line segments, three angles and three vertices.

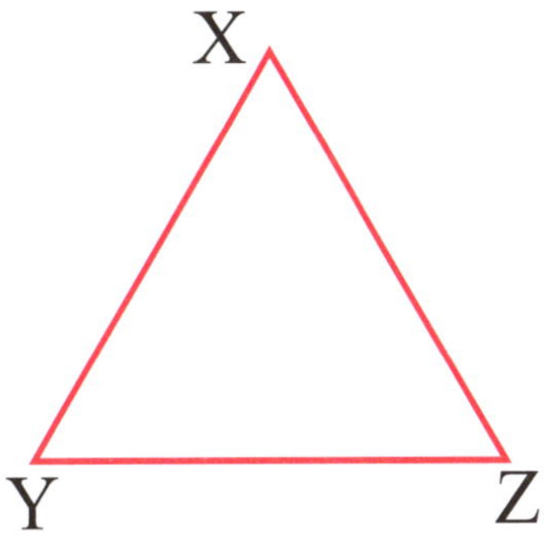

XYZ is a triangle.

XYZ has 3 sides XY, YZ AND XZ

$\triangle$ XYZ has 3 angles $\angle$XYZ, $\angle$XZY

$\triangle$ XYZ has 3 vertices X, Y, Z

[Remember vertex is a point.]

Classification of Triangles

According to sides

1. Equilateral triangle

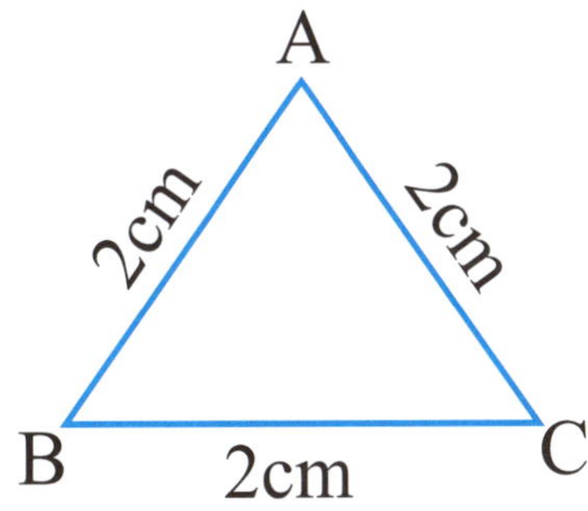

If all sides of a triangle are of equal length, it is an equilateral triangle.

(Measure each angle of this triangle)

2. Isosceles triangle

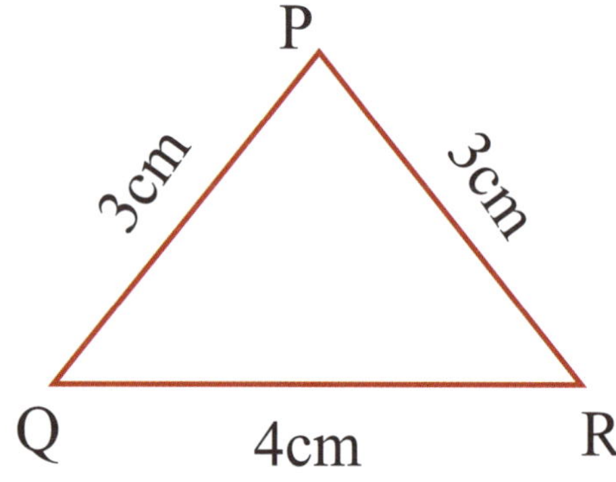

If two opposite sides are of equal length, such a triangle is called an isosceles triangle.

(Measure the 3 angles.)

3. Scalene triangle

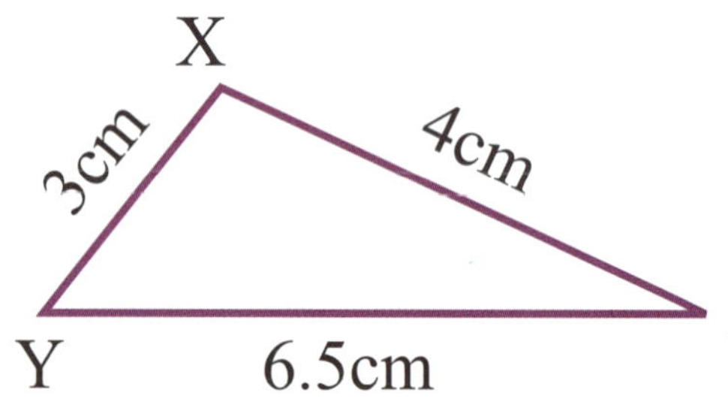

If all three sides of a triangle are of different length it is called a scalene triangle.

(Measure the angles)

According to angles

When all 3 angles of a triangle are acute angles (less than 90°) it is an **acute angled triangle**. When one angle of a triangle is a right angle (90°) it is a **right angled triangle**.

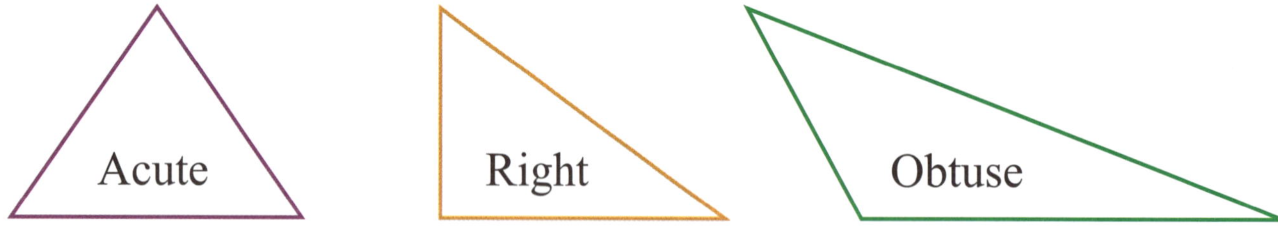

When angle of a triangle is an obtuse angle (greater than 90°) it is an **obtuse angled triangle**.

Exercise 7.5

1. Classify the following triangles with respect to their sides.

a.

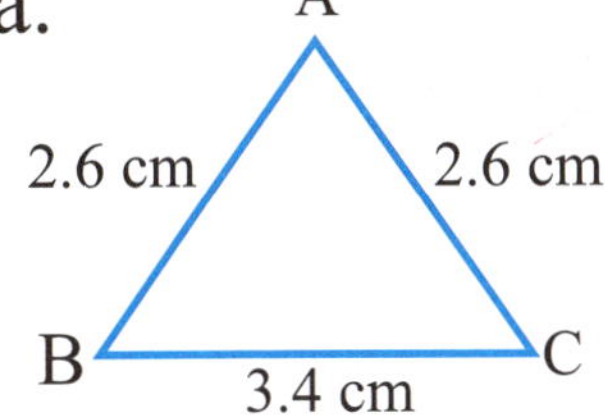

b.

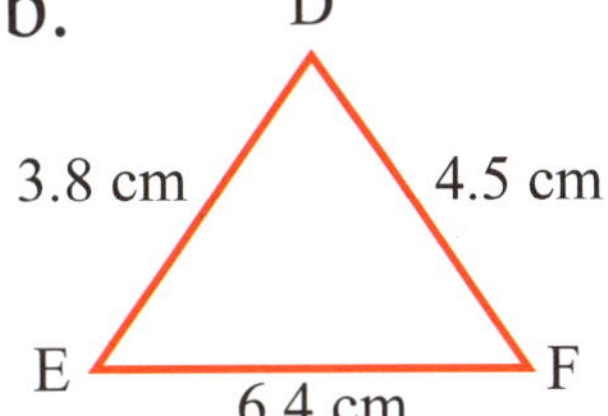

c.

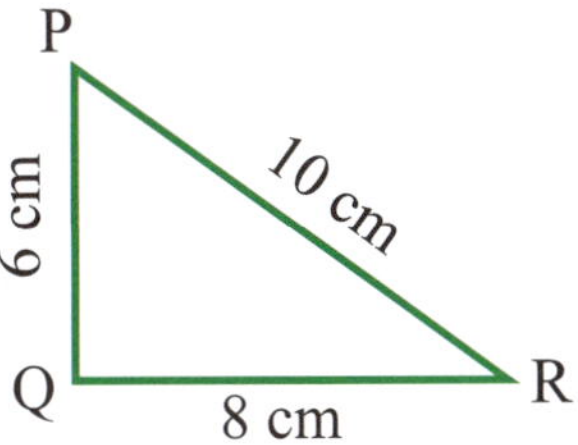

2. Classify the following triangles with respect to their angles.

a.

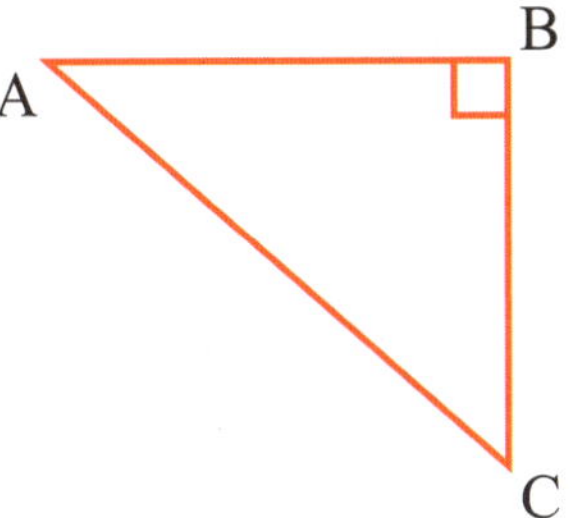

b.

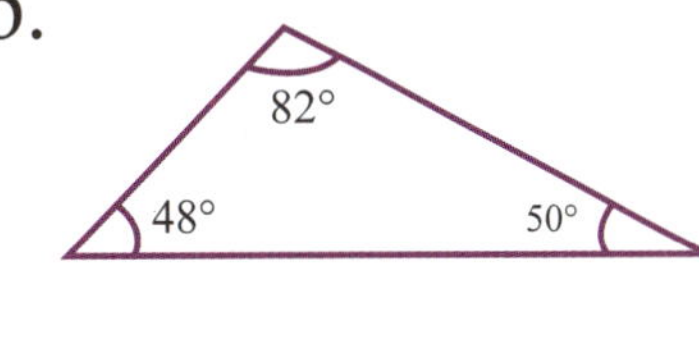

c.

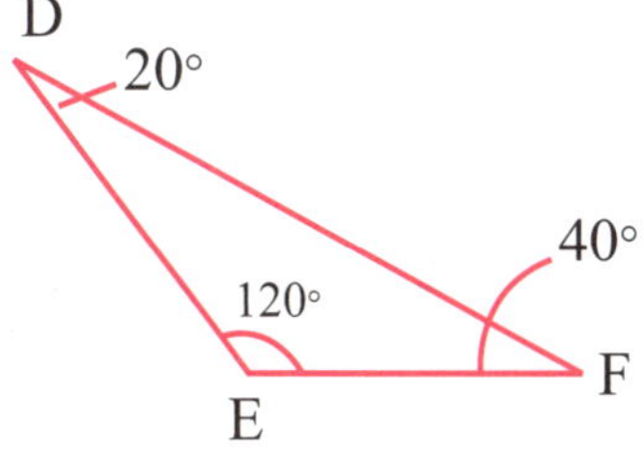

Quadrilaterals

A four sided polygon is called a quadrilateral ('Quad' means four and 'lateral' means sides.)

Some special kinds of quadrilaterals:

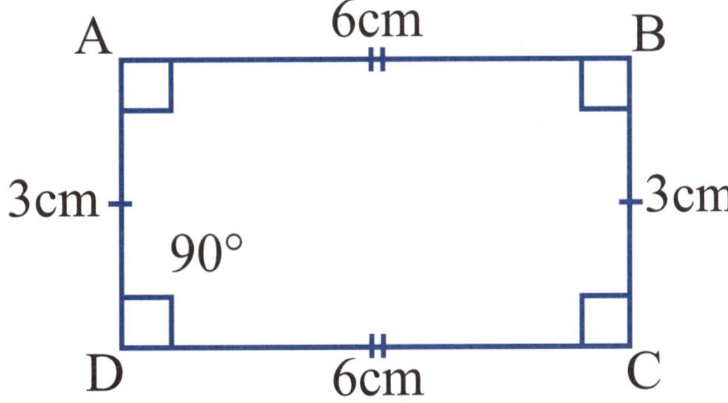

Rectangle

All angles are 90°each. Opposite sides are parallel. Opposite sides are equal.

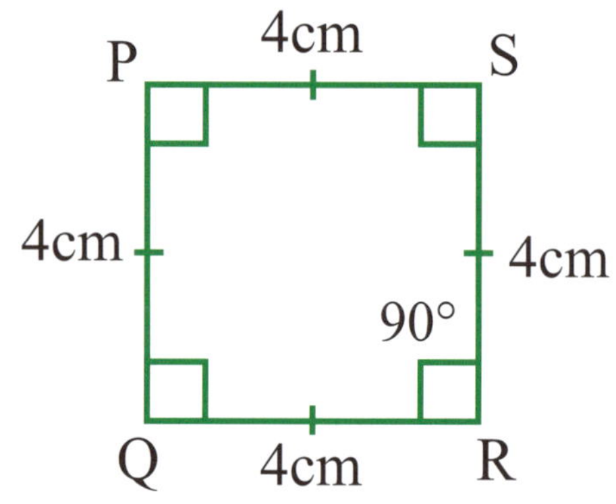

Square

All angles are right angles (90°)

All sides are equal. Opposite sides are parallel.

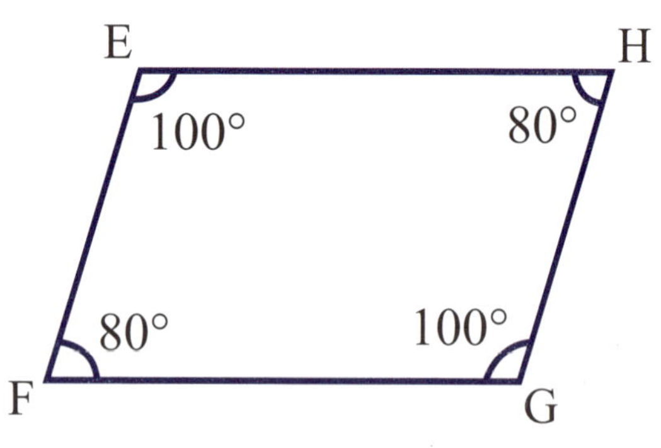

Parallelogram

Opposite sides are parallel and equal. Only opposite angles are equal.

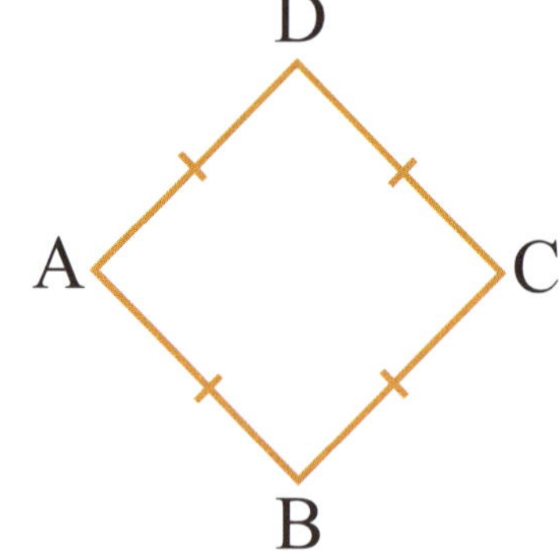

Rhombus

Opposite sides are parallel, all sides are equal.

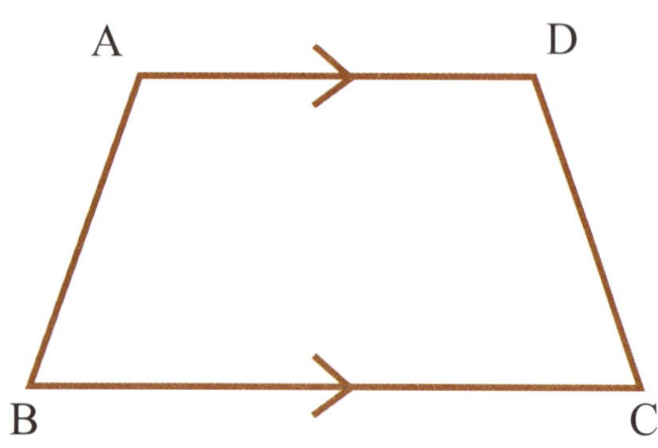

Trapezium

One pair of opposite sides are parallel.

Exercise 7.6

1. Join the dots to draw rectangles, square, rhombus, parallelogram and a trapezium & name them.

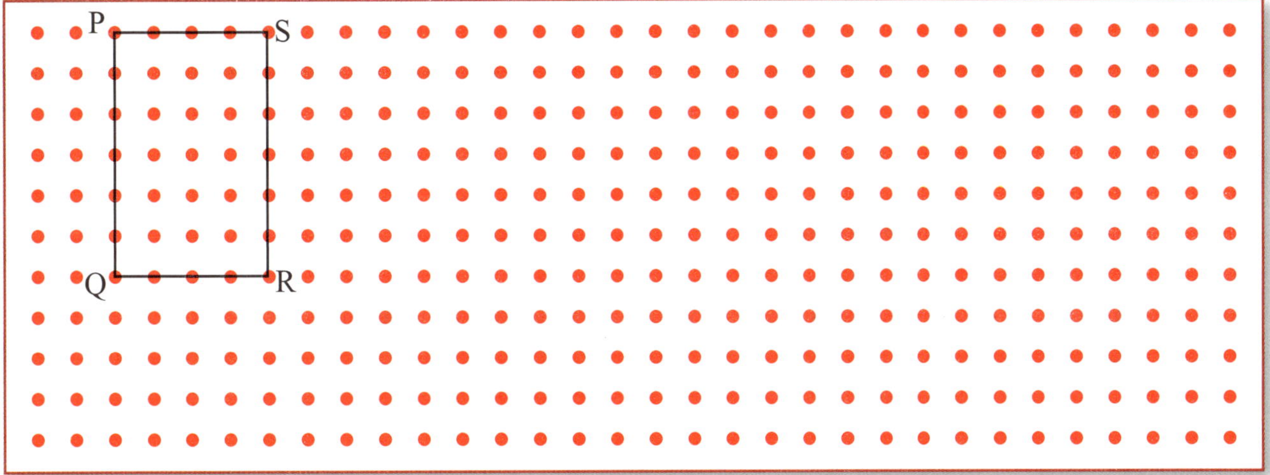

2. Fill in the blanks

   a. A quadrilateral in which all sides are equal is a ______ or ______

   b. ______ and ______ have opposite sides parallel and equal.

   c. Quadrilaterals in which each angle is 90 degree are ______ and ______.

   d. In a ______ only one pair of sides are parallel.

Circles

We have studied about circles in our previous class. Let us quickly recapitulate what we had learnt.

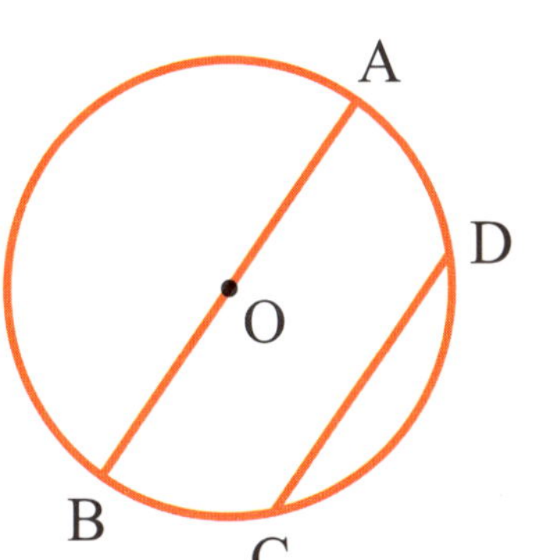

O is the centre.

OA = radius

AB = 2× radius

= Diameter

CD is a chord

AB is the longest chord.

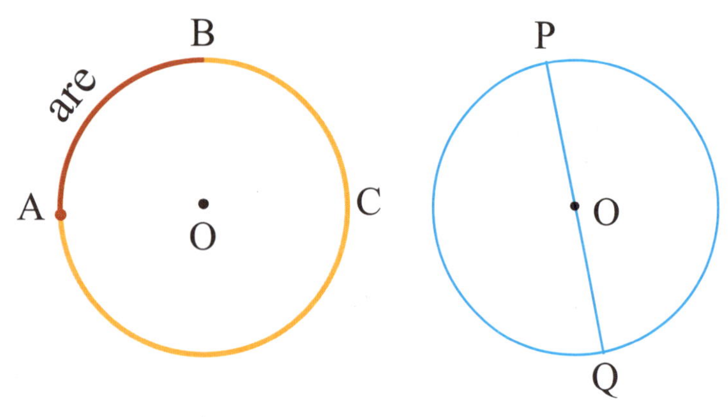

A part of the circle is an arc. The distance around the circle is called the circumference. Half a circle is semi circle. A diameter cuts a circle into 2 halves or 2 semi circles.

Measuring diameter

XY = diameter = OX + OY (All radii of a circle are equal)

= 2 radius

= 2×2 cm

= 4 cm

Radius = $\frac{1}{2}$ diameter

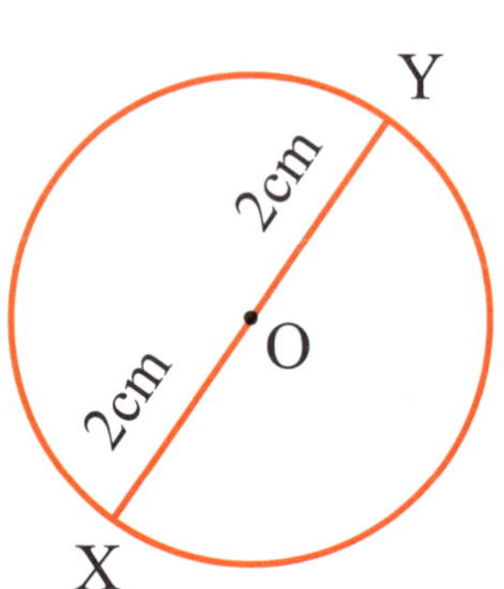

 **Exercise 7.7**

1. Complete the table

Radius (in cm)	2.5			10.5	3.6		0.6
Diameter (in cm)		7	4.8			8.4	

2. See the figure and name the following.

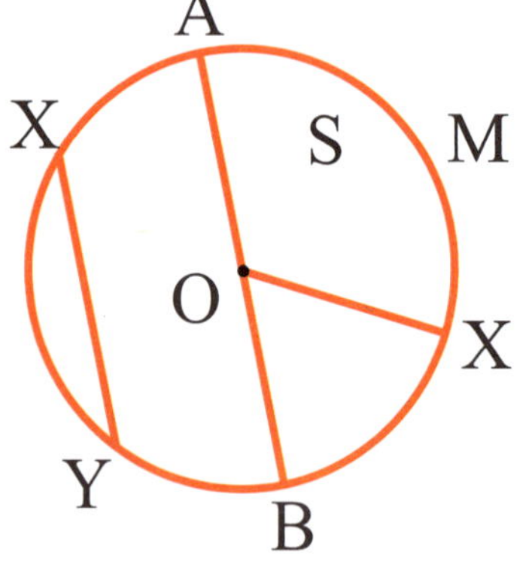

Centre ______

Diameter ______

3 radii ______, ______, ______

2 chords ______, ______,

Mental Maths

1. State whether the following statements are true or false

   a. An angle whose measure is greater than 90° is an acute angle.

   b. A circle can have only one diameter.

   c. A ray has only one end point.

   d. A line has 2 end points.

   e. Radius of a circle is one half of its diameter.

2. Fill in the blanks

   a. The mid point of a diameter of a circle is the _______ of the circle.

   b. Half a circle is called a _______.

   c. If radius of a circle is 3.5cm, its diameter is _______ cm.

   d. Measure of a straight angle is ________.

   e. A ________ has definite length.

8

Area and Volume

There are two boards in the class room. One in a black board and other is a display board.

Which board is covering more surface?

Blackboard covers more surface than the display board. So, we can say, area of blackboard is greater than the area of the display board.

So, **area of a shape** or a closed figure is the amount of surface covered by it.

How to measure area

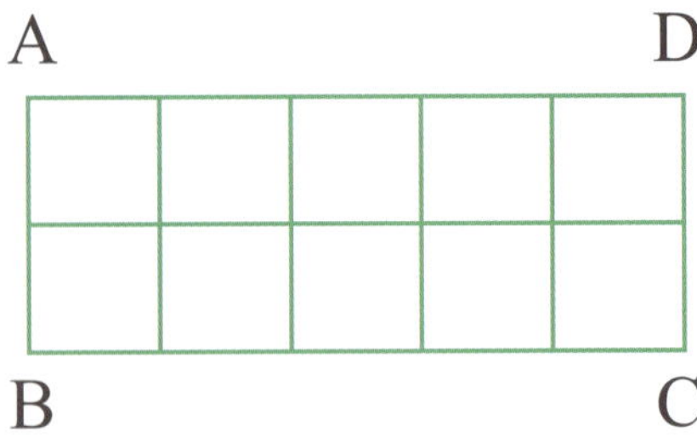

The rectangle ABCD has 10 squares. We can say area of the rectangle is 10 squares.

Which figures have area 6 squares?

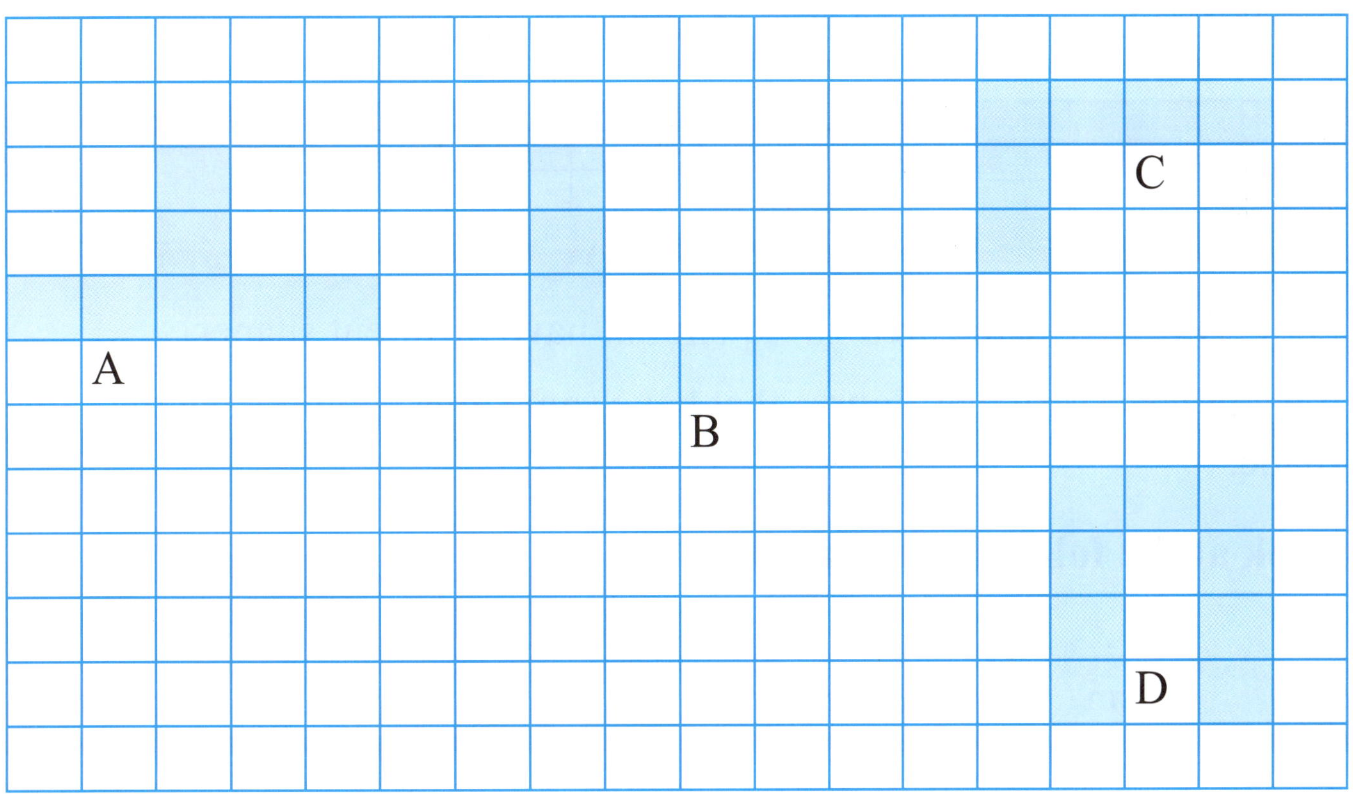

Just as we take 1 cm or 1 m as a unit for measuring length of any line, in the above examples we use 'squares' as unit for expressing areas.

The square can be a square centimeter or a square metre or any other square unit of length.

1cm
1cm 1 sq 1cm
1cm

It is a square centimeter or sq cm when each side of the square is 1 cm. A square metre or any other square unit of length.

Area of figure is 12 sq cm

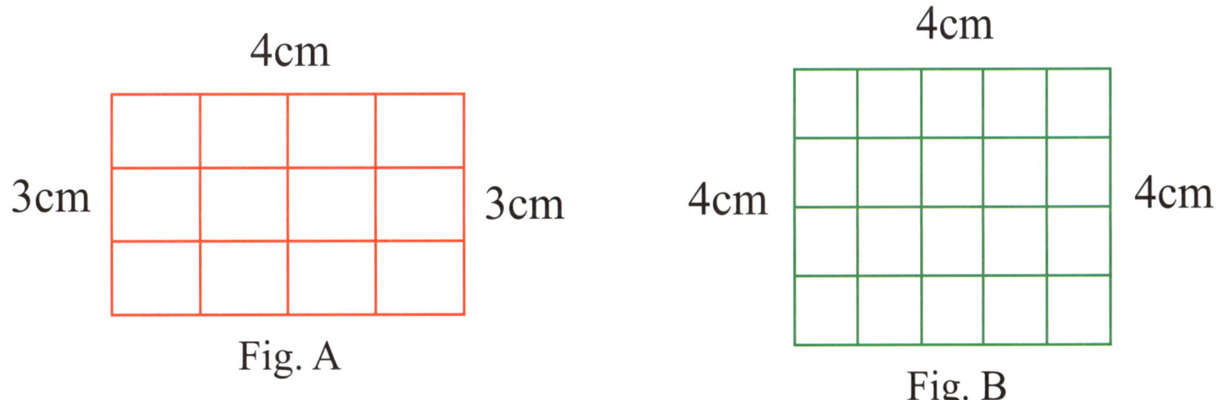

Fig. A

Fig. B

Area of figure B = $4 \times 4 = 16$ sq cm

Hence, we see area of a rectangle or a square is equal to the product of its length and breadth. It is expressed in square units.

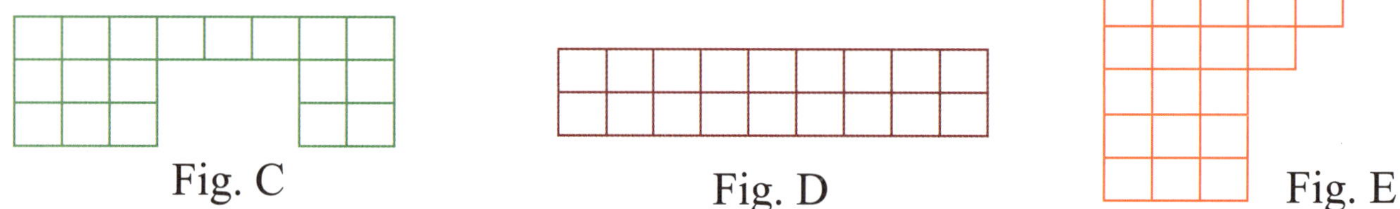

Fig C,D,E have same area 18 Sq cm but have different shapes.

It is not necessary that figures that have same area should have the same shape.

Look at the following rectangles.

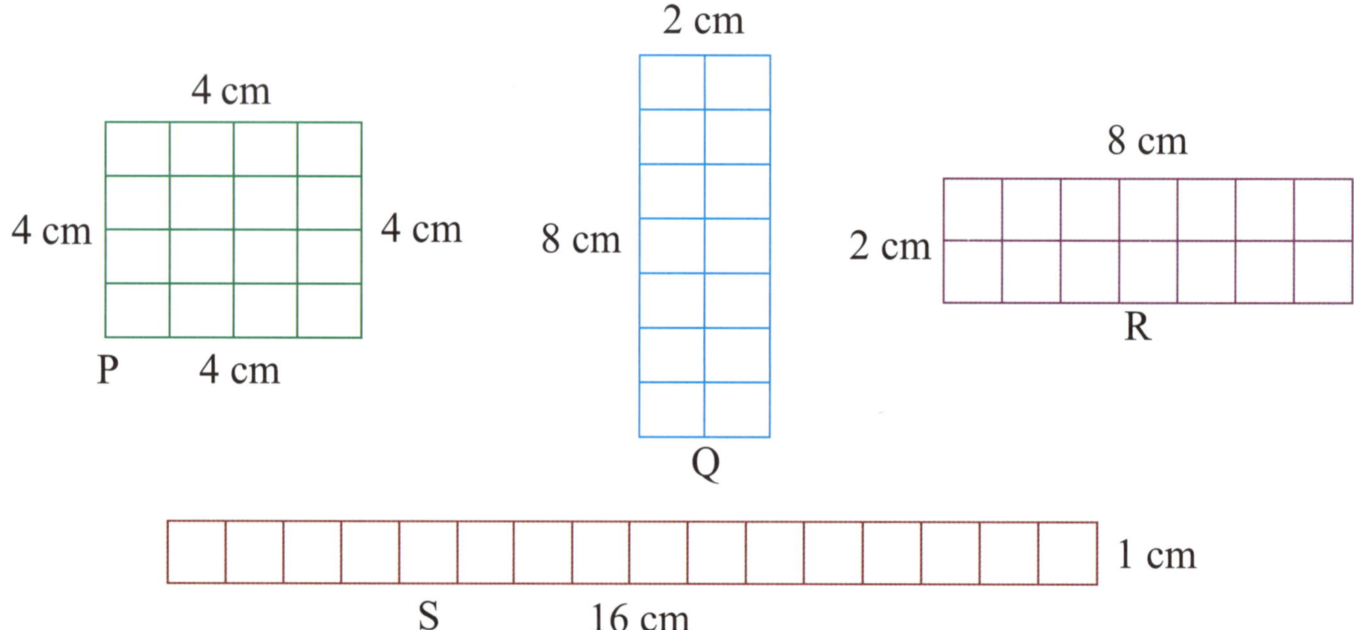

All the 4 rectangles P, Q, R, S have area 16sq cm

Rectangle P ⟶ 4cm × 4cm = 16 sq cm

Rectangle Q ⟶ 8cm × 2 cm = 16 sq cm

Rectangle R ⟶ 2 cm × 8cm = 16 sq cm

Rectangle S ⟶ 16 cm × 1 cm = 16 sq cm

The length and breadth of the rectangles are factors of 16.

So, we see a given area can have different lengths and breadths.

Exercise 8.1

1. Find the area of the following.

1 2 3

4 5 6

2. Find the area of these rectangles (and squares)

5 cm

1 cm

6 cm

2 cm

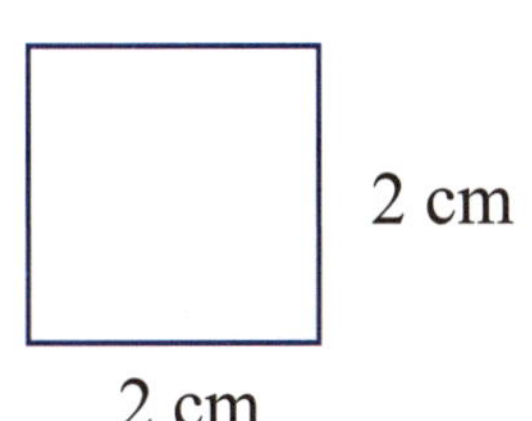

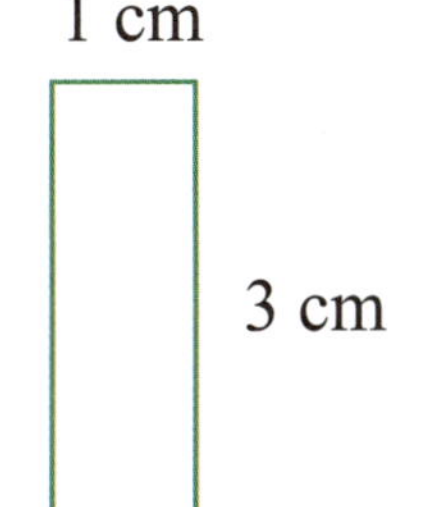

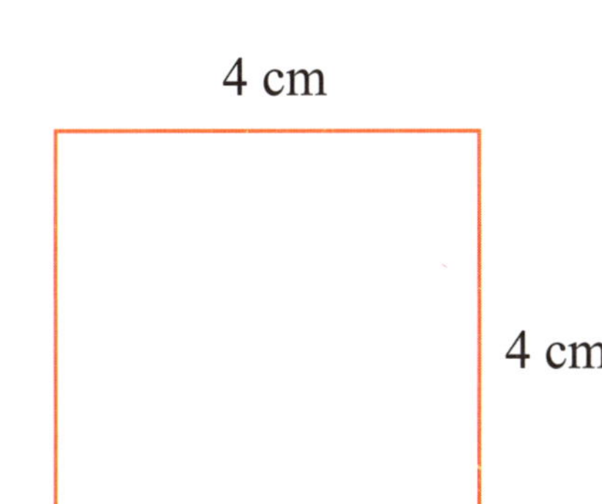

3. Find the areas of these figures by dividing them into rectangles and squares.

a.

1 cm
a 1 cm
3 cm b 1 cm
c 1 cm
3 cm

Divide it into squares and rectangles as of a + b + c

$(1 \times 1) + (2 \times 1) + (3 \times 1)$

$1 + 2 + 3 = 6$ sq cm

b.

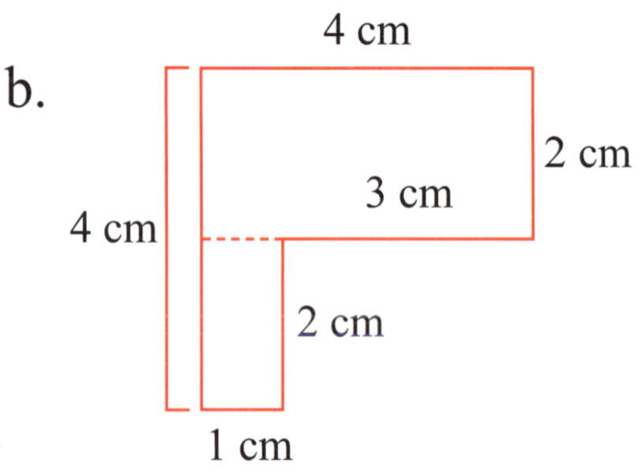

c.

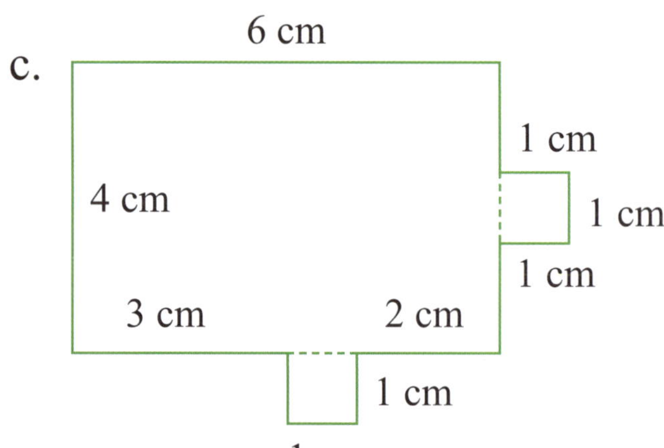

d.

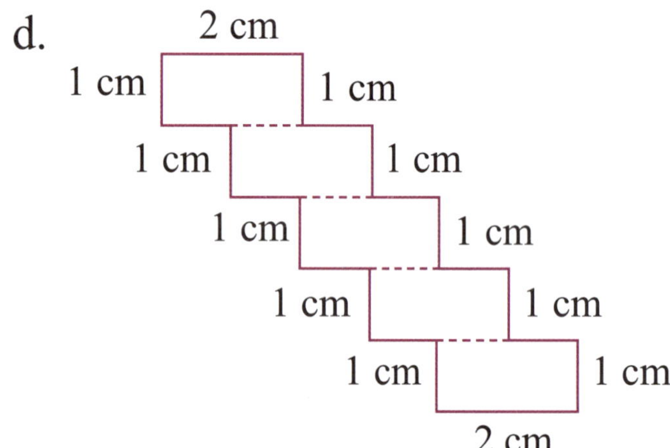

Area of irregular plane surfaces or when whole squares are not covered

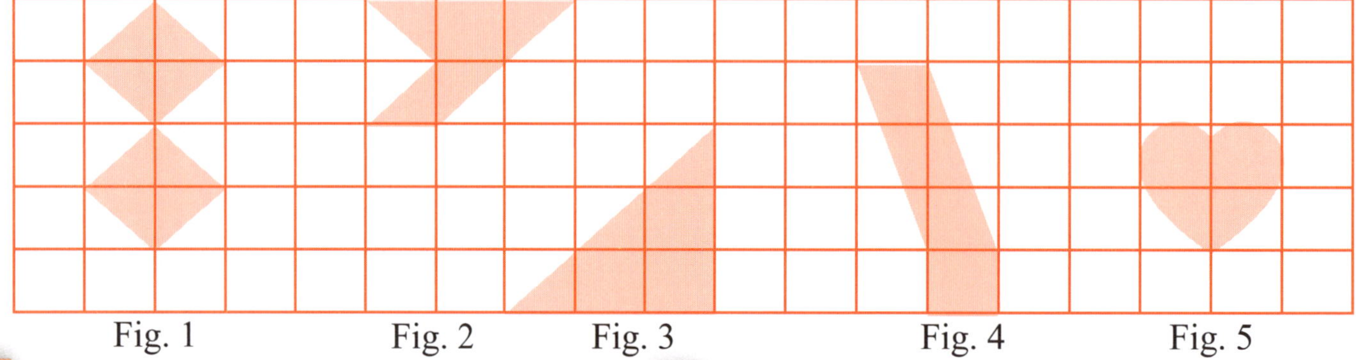

Fig. 1 Fig. 2 Fig. 3 Fig. 4 Fig. 5

When figures do not cover a square completely we follow these rules:

1. Count full squares enclosed.
2. If the figure covers half a square it is taken as half.
3. When more than half a square is covered, count it as a whole square.
4. Do not count less than half a square.

So, by this method

Area of figure 1 is 4 sq cm

Area of figure 2 is 3 sq cm

Area of figure 3 is 4.5 sq cm

Area of figure 4 is 4 sq cm (approximate)

Area of figure 5 is 3 sq cm (approximate)

Exercise 8.2

1. Find the area of the following figures in the centimetre grid.

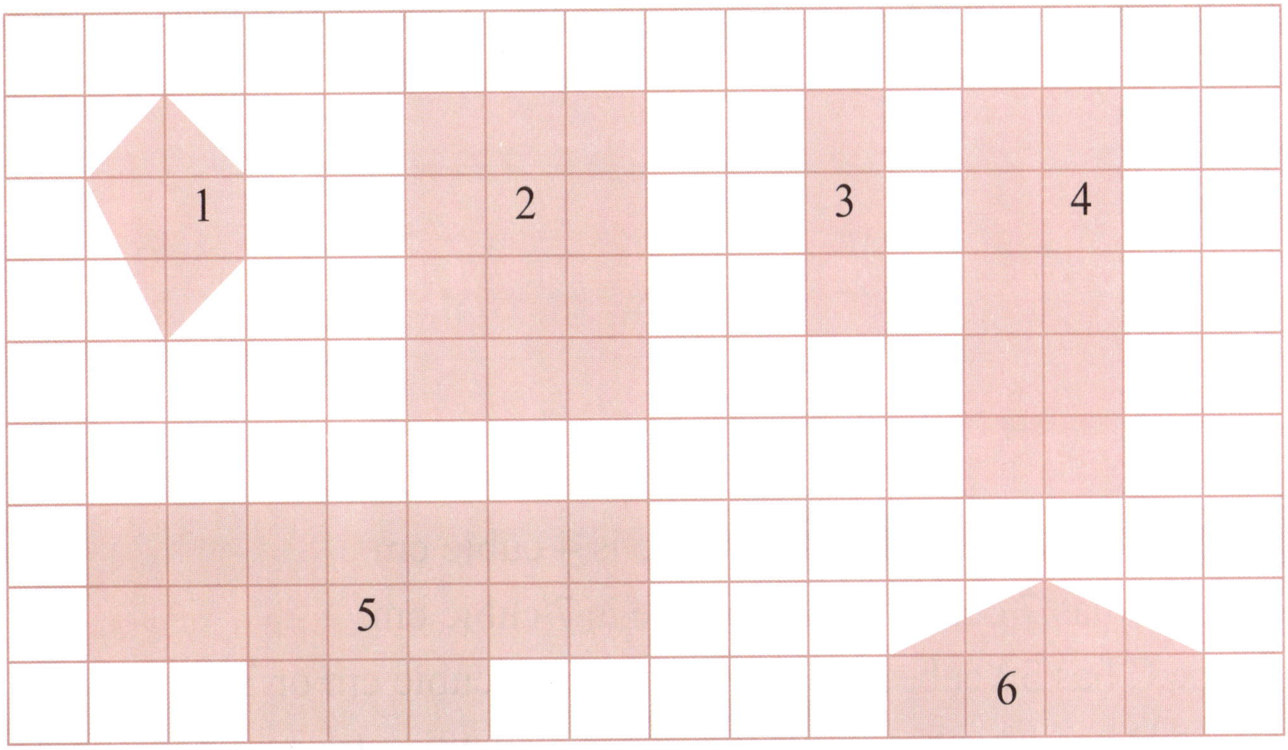

1 2 3 4

5

6

Word Problems

1. A rectangle is 4.5 cm long and 3.5 cm broad. Find its area.
2. Find the area of the room, which is 8.5 cm long and 6 m broad.
3. What is the area of a square park of side 100 m? Find the cost of planting grass in this park at the rate of ₹ 15 per square meter.
4. A prayer room is 15 m long and 10 m wide. How many square tiles of side 5 m will be required to cover the floor of the room?

Volume

We know solids occupy space.

The amount of space a solid occupies is its volume.

A cube is a solid. This cube has length = 1 cm

Breadth = 1cm

Height = 1 cm.

Its volume is equal to 1 cubic cm or 1 cm^3. Look at these shapes and tell how many centimeter cubes are used to make them.

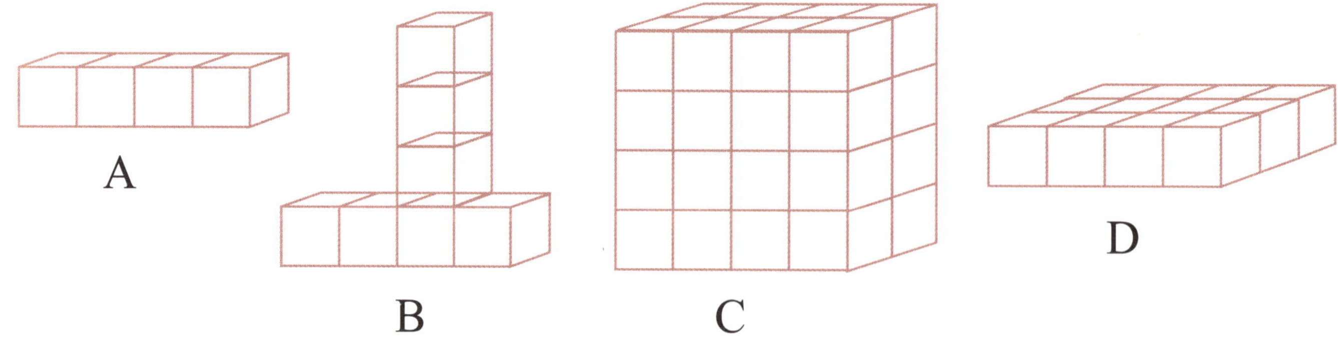

Shape A has 4 cubes, so its volume is 4 cubic cm.

Shape B has 7 cubes, so its volume is 7 cubic cm.

Shape C has 32 cubes, so its volume is 32 cubic cm or 32 cube cm

Shape D has 12 cubes, so its volume is 12 centimetre cm or 12 cubic cm

Volume of a cuboid

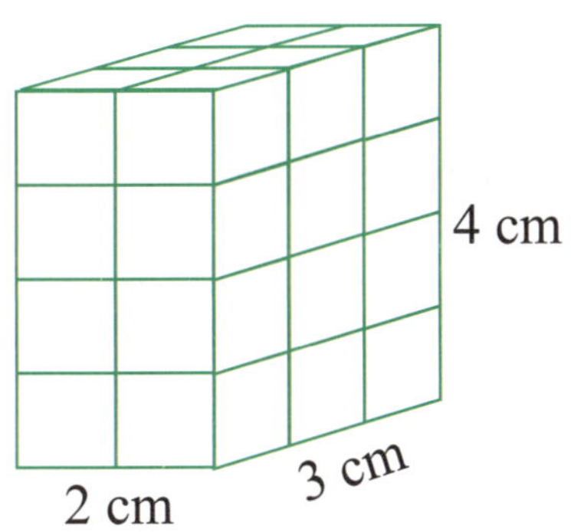

This is the shape of a cuboid which is made up of 18 cubes so its volume is 18 cm cube.

length = 2 cm, breadth = 3 cm, height = 4 cm

$l \times b \times h = 2 \times 3 \times 4$

= 24 cubc^1 cm or 24 cm^3

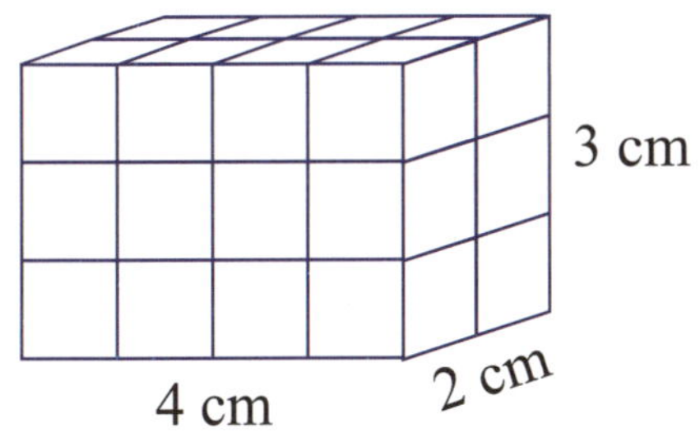

Therefore volume of cuboid = $l \times b \times h$

Volume of the cuboid = 24 cubc^1 cm

$l \times b \times h = 4 \times 2 \times 3 = v = 24$

Volume of a cube

A cube has length = breadth = height

So, volume of a cube = $l \times l \times l$

Exercise 8.3

1. Find the volume of each figure given below.

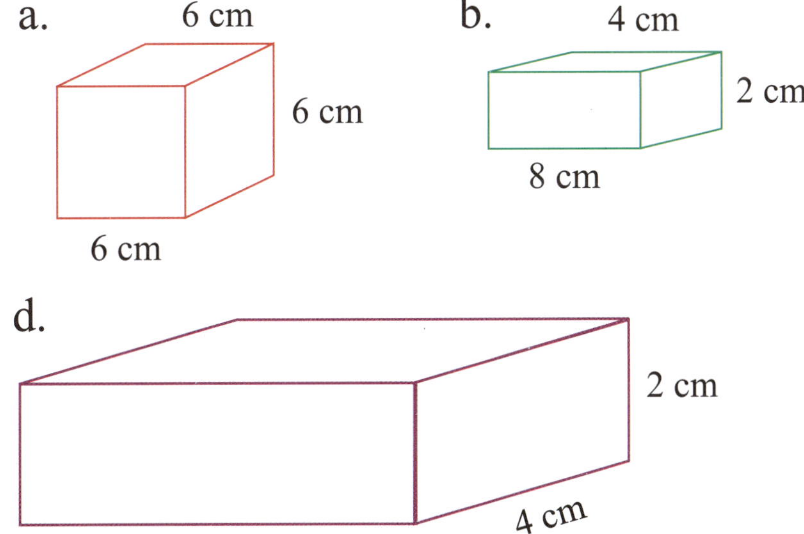

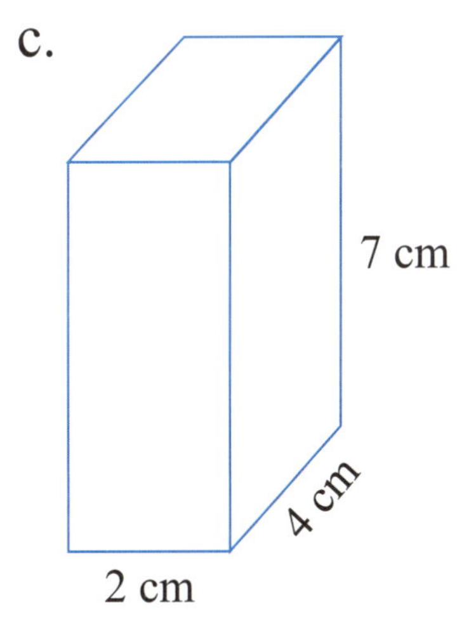

2. Find the volume of cubes of the following dimensions.

a. 5cm b. 4.5 cm c. 10 cm d. 12.5 cm e. 2.7 cm

3. Find the volume of the cuboids of the following dimensions.

a. length = 8 cm breadth = 3 cm height = 5 cm

b. length = 4.5 cm breadth = 6 cm height = 3 cm

c. length = 10 cm breadth = 3.5 cm height = 4.5 cm

d. length = 2.3 cm breadth = 1.2 cm height = 3.8 cm

4. A swimming pool is 25 m long, 18 m broad and 2 m deep. What is the volume of the pool?

5. Find the volume of the box which is 1.2 m long, 0.8 m wide and 1.5 m deep.

Lab Activity

Here are some NETS. Make the figures with the following.

1. Cuboid

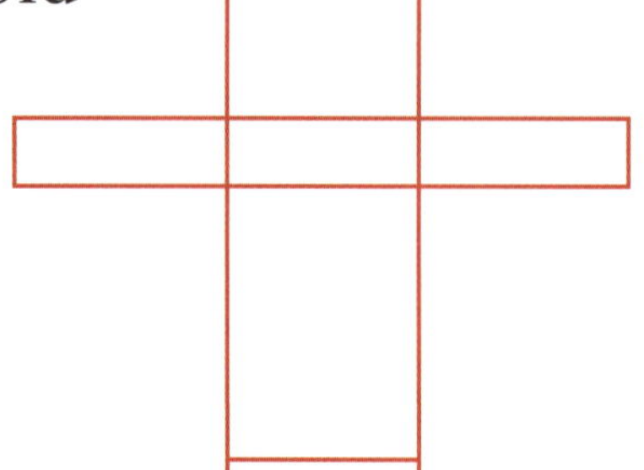

2. Cube

3. Cut and fold along dotted lines, see what is formed.

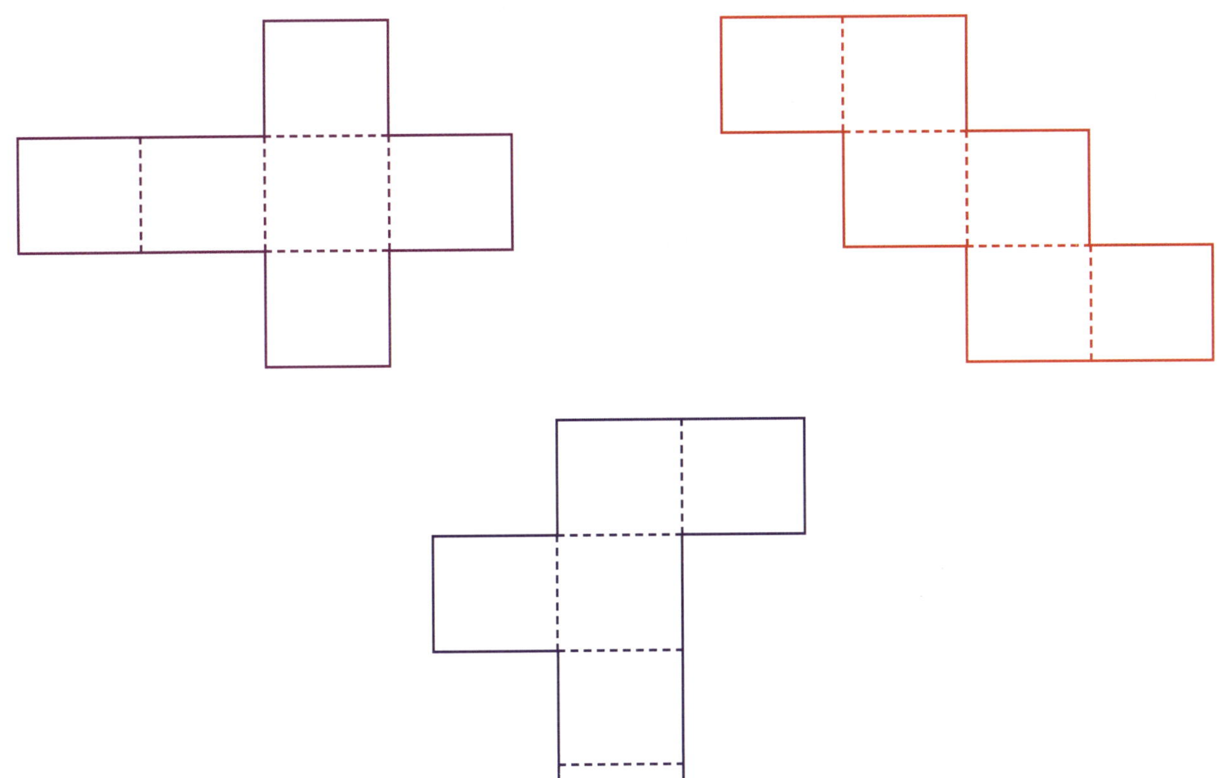

If each square is of side 2 cm, what is the volume of each cube you get?

Mental Maths

1. Choose the correct answer

   a. Volume of a cube of edge 1 cm is

   (i) 1 cm^3 (ii) 3 cm^3 (iii) 6 cm^3

   b. The unit of volume is

   (i) sq units (ii) unit of length (iii) cubic

   c. The area and perimeter of one if the following squares is numerically the same. Which are is it?

   (i) A square of side 2 cm

   (ii) A square of side 3 cm

   (iii) A square of side 4 cm

   d. Area of a square is 121 sq cm. Its side measures

   (i) 9 cm (ii) 10 cm (iii) 11 cm

2. Find the area of

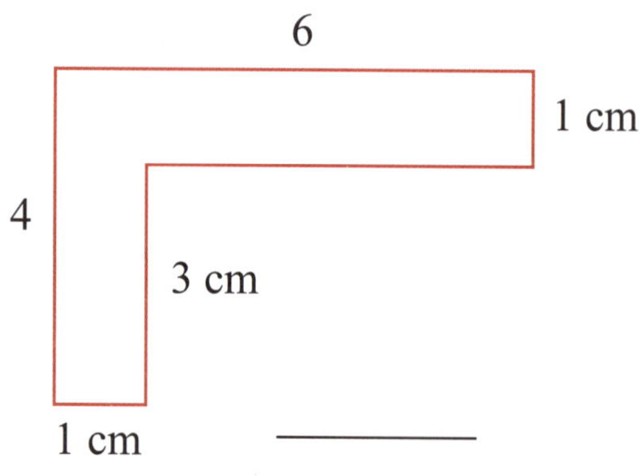

______

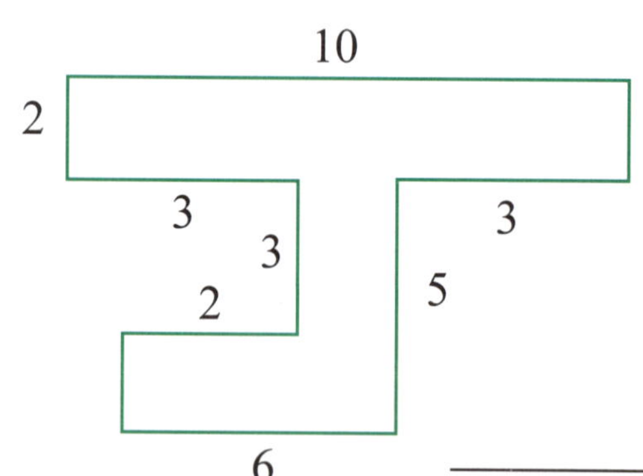

______

Averages & Temperature

9

Sumit's score in the tests is....

	Out of 20
English	18
Maths	20
Hindi	15
EVS	15
Total	68

If he had scored say 17 in all subjects.

E	17
M	17
H	17
EVS	17
TOTAL	68

Then also the total remains the same. We can say he has an average of 17

To find the average of a group of numbers, we

1. Find the sum of all the numbers in the group, and then
2. Divide the sum by the total number in the group.

EXAMPLE

Sachin scroed 102, 98, 4 and 66 in 4 innings. Find his batting average.

Solution: Total score = 102 + 98 + 14 + 66 = 280

Total number of innings played = 4

$\therefore$ Average score = $\frac{\text{Total scorein 4 innings}}{\text{total no. of innings}} = \frac{280}{4} = 70$

So, Sachin's batting average is 70. (Averages are used for comparison in the field of education, sports, economy etc. There is a branch of mathematics called statistics, where averages are used.)

Let us see how averages will help us to compare.

EXAMPLE

The weekly consumption of sugar in 4 weeks by two families is given.

	Sharmas	**Guptas**
Week 1	4 kg	5 kg
Week 2	5 kg	3.5 kg
Week 3	3.5 kg	4.5 kg
Week 4	4.5 kg	5 kg

Compare the quantities of sugar consumed by the two families.

Solution:	**Sharmas**	**Guptas**
Total	17 kg	26 kg

Average consumption = $\frac{\text{Total consumption}}{\text{Total number of weeks}}$

Per week for Sharmas $= \frac{17}{4} = 4.25$ kg

Per week for Guptas $= \frac{18}{4} = 4.5$ kg

Hence, we see the average weekly consumption of sugar by the Guptas is more than that of Sharmas.

Exercise 9.1

1. In a mango grove, 4 trees produced 90, 82, 95 and 88 mangoes. What is the average number of mangoes each tree produced?

2. Find the average rainfall in a certain city for a week, if the actual rainfall for the week is as follows:

Day	Mon	Tue	Wed	Thu	Fri	Sat	Sun
Rain fall (In cm)	4.1	5.2	4.6	6	7.5	8	8

3. Find the average of

   a. 18, 24, 32, 48

   b. 1.1, 2.2, 3.3, 4.4, 5.5

   c. 98, 86, 84, 72, 85

4. Find the averages of first 10 counting numbers.

5. Find the average number of students in a section of class V, if no. of students in 5 sections are 40, 42, 39, 37 and 40 respectively.

6.

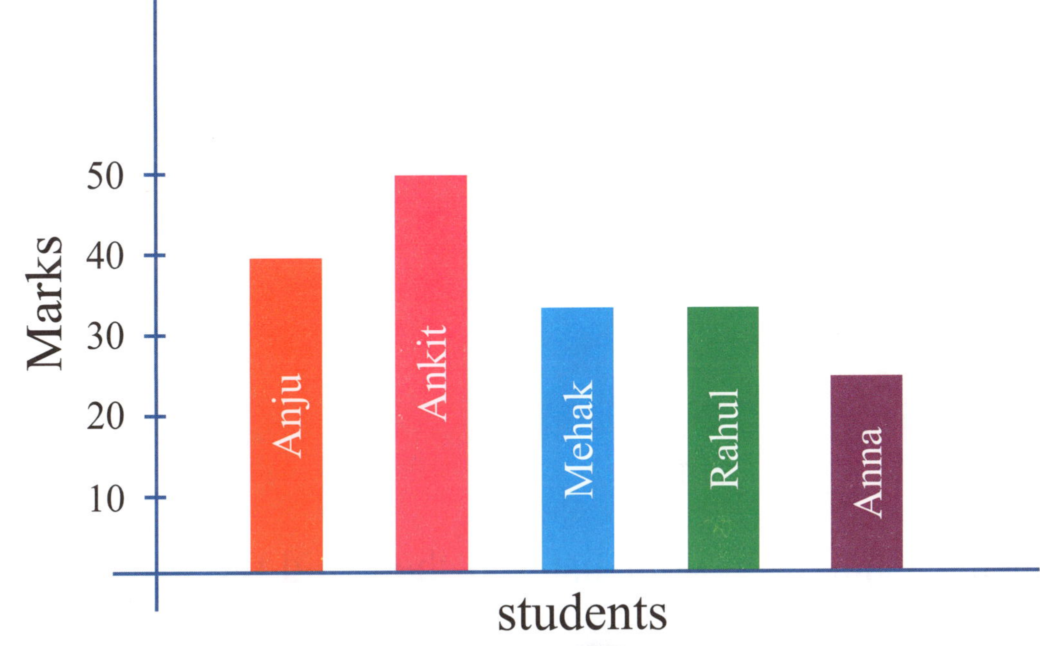

The bar graph shows the marks obtained by these 5 students in a Maths test (out of 50)

a. Find the average.

b. How many students got above average?

c. How many students got less than the average marks?

Lab Activity

1. Collect data of weight of 6 of your classmates and find the average weight.

Name							
Weight (in kg)							

Average weight ________

2. Collect the data of temperature during the week and find the average.

Day	Mon	Tue	Wed	Thu	Fri	Sat	Sun
Temp (°C)							

Average ________ °C

3. Collect data of height of 8 of your friends, and find their average height (include yourself)

Name							
Height (cm)							

Average height________cm

Add your teacher's height to your list and then find the average height again.

Unitary Method

I went to a shop to buy 3 pens. The shopkeeper told me the cost of a dozen pens was ₹ 60, I gave him ₹ 50 and he returned ₹ 35. On my way back I was trying to calculate how he arrived at the cost of 3 pens, so quickly. I reached home and asked my Father. He said, "Its simple, cost of a dozen pens is ₹ 60, how will you find cost of 1 pen?" I said, "Oh, I know that! Divide 60 by 12. It's ₹ 5 per pen." Then he said. "Now what will be the cost of 3 such pens?" I replied immediately "₹ 15"

So, my father explained that this is called the **unitary method**. In this method the cost of 1 object is found and then cost of many objects is calculated by multiplying cost of 1 object with the number of objects.

$$\text{Cost of 1 object.} = \frac{\text{Cost of (serveral) given number number of objects}}{\text{Number of objects}}$$

Cost of required number of objects = Cost of 1 object × required number of objects

EXAMPLE

Cost of 8 bags is ₹ 336. Find the cost of 3 bags.

Solution: These problems are done in two steps.

1st step: cost of 1 bag is to be found.

Cost of 1 bag = Cost of 8 bags ÷ 8

$= ₹\ \frac{336}{8}$

$= ₹\ 42$

2nd step: cost of 3 bags = (Cost of 1 bag) × 3

$= ₹\ 42 \times 3$

$= ₹\ 126$

Exercise 9.2

1. Cost of 1 dozen eggs is ₹ 24. Find the cost of 30 eggs.
2. The weight of 20 bags of rice is 380 kg. Find the cost of 150 bags of rice.
3. A machine can print 340 pages in 5 hours. If 408 pages have to be printed. How many hours will the machine take?
4. The distance covered by a train in 11 hours is 605 km. What is the distance covered by the train in 7 hours?
5. Rahul spends ₹ 15600 in one year. How much money does he spend in 7 months?
6. A factory produces 82440 bulbs in the month of April. How many bulbs will be produced in 6 days? (assume same number is produced everyday)

Help Mr. Chang

Mr Chang is a chef. He is unwell and his assistant Ping has to cook and serve guests. He is confused. Help him.

Recipe for fruit squash (one of the items)

Ingredients

1. 200 g Chopped oranges
2. 1000 ml lemonade
3. 500 ml Orange juice
4. 4 orange rings
5. 8 ice cubes

Method

Mix all ingredients, except ice cubes. Take 4 tall glasses. Pour the ingredients. Add 2 ice cubes per glass. Add orange slice as decoration and serve.

Help Ping find out the amount of each of the ingredients for making fruit squash for

1. 8 people
2. 9 people
3. 12 people
4. 50 people
5. 75 people

Temperature

After learning measures like length, mass, capacity and time let's learn another important measure that is temperature.

The hotness or coldness of an object is expressed by its **temperature** and the instrument used to measure it, is **thermometer**.

Temperature is measured in degree Fahrenheit (°F) and in degree Celsius (°C) so, thermometers have scales in degree Fahrenheit or degree Celsius. Celsius scale also called centigrade scale, is marked from 0° to 100°. 0° shows the freezing point of water and 100° shows the boiling point of water.

The Fahrenheit scale is marked from 32° to 212° where 32°F shows the freezing point of water and 212°F shows boiling point of water.

	°C	°F
Freezing point of water	0°	32°
Boiling point of water	100°	212°
Normal body temp	37°	98.6°

Shows comparison of °C & °F

Conversion

From °C to °F $[°C \times 9] \div 5 + 32 = °F$

EXAMPLE

Convert 35°C to Fahrenheit scale

Solution : 35° × 9 = 315°

315 ÷ 5 = 63 + 32 = 95°F

From °F to °C

[°F – 32] × 5 ÷ 9 = °C

EXAMPLE

Convert 122°F to Celsius scale

Solution : 122°F – 32 = 90

90 × 5 = 450

450 ÷ 9 = 50°C Ans

Exercise 9.3

1. Convert the temperatures given in Celsius scale to Fahrenheit scale.

   a. 20°C b. 30°C c. 0°C

   d. 80°C e. 40°C f. 100°C

2. Convert the temperatures to Celsius scale.

   a. 86°F b. 113°F c. 194°F

   d. 158°F e. 95°F f. 140°F

3. A sick person having 103°F temperature took some medicine. This temperature dropped by 3°F. What is the temperature in °C?

4. Maximum temp of a day is 35°C and minimum temperature is 25°C. What is the difference in the Fahrenheit scale?

Hang a thermometer in the classroom. Let the students record the room temperature in the morning and afternoon for the week.

They should find the average morning temperature and average noon temperature. They can convert it to fahrenheit scale.

The temperature of a healty human body is 98.6° F. So, if a person is suffering from fever his body temperature will be above 98.6°F. A Clinical thermometer is used to measure the temperature of human body. It is marked in °C or °F.

The shining liquid in the thermometer is mercury. When the thermometer is in contact with a body which is hot the mercury expands and rises. The number in degree against which column rises and stops, indicates the temperature of the person.

Mental Maths

1. Fill in the blanks

a. Average of 0.2, 0, 2 and 0.002 is __________.

b. Average of first five odd numbers is __________.

c. Average of first five prime numbers is _________.

d. The average of $7\frac{1}{2}, 9\frac{3}{4}, 15\frac{2}{3}$ is ________.

e. The table shows the marks (out of 100) in various subject

Subjects	English	Hindi	Maths	Science
Marks	75	70	85	64

His average marks are __________.

The attendance of sections of class V during the week is

Class	Mon	Tue	Wed	Thu	Fri
VA	42	40	38	33	39
VB	40	42	36	37	41
VC	38	36	34	35	40
VD	40	38	38	33	40

a. Which section has the best average during the week?

b. Which section has the poorest average?

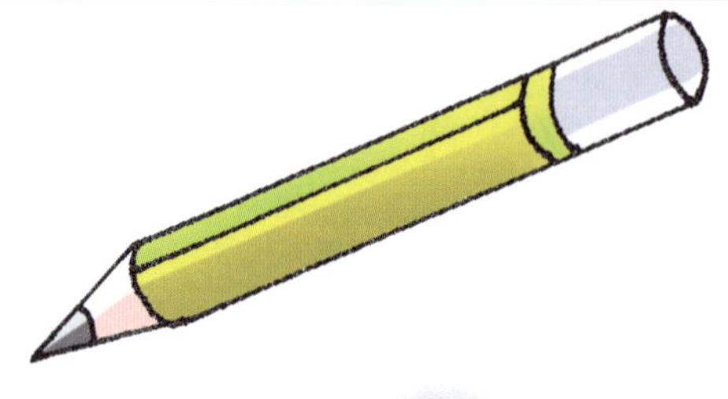

10

Percentages

The term percent comes from two latin words ‘per centum’ which means “out of 100”.

If we take a grid of 10 × 10 squares and shade say, 35 ,then we can say that the shaded part is 35 out of 100 or 35 per cent of the whole.The symbol used for representing percentage is ‘%’

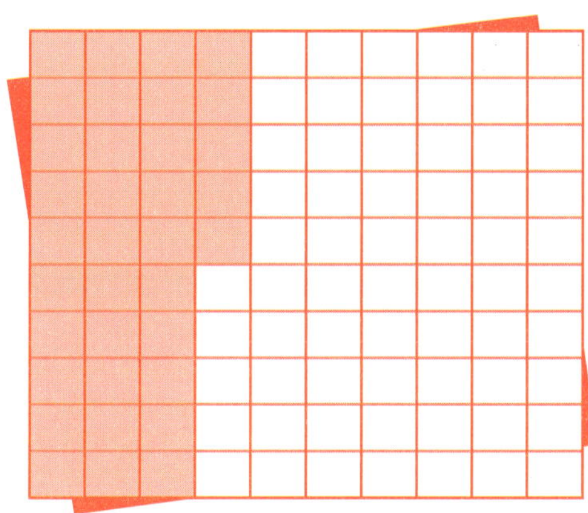

Shaded portion is $\frac{35}{100}$ 35 %

Hence, we can say 1 square in the grid containing 100 squares represents 1 %.

We will use the 10 × 10 grid to understand the concept of percentages.

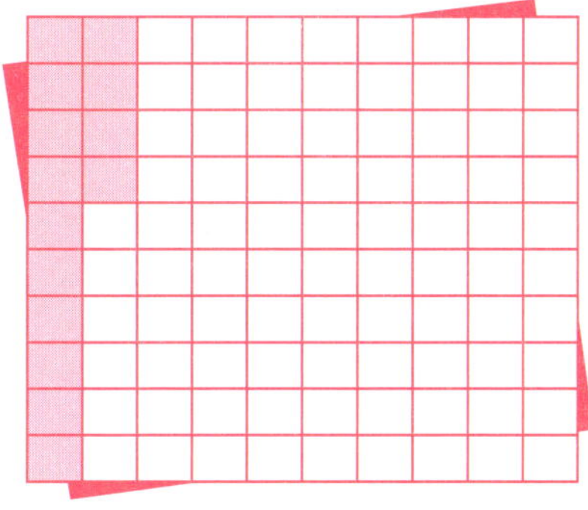

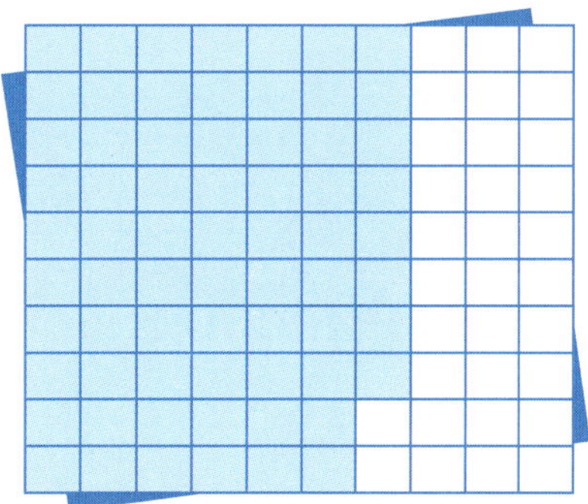

Shaded : 14 out of 100 = 14 %

Shaded ------------------------------%

Unshaded 86 out of 100 = 86 %

Unshaded --------------------------%

Shade 1 %, 94 % and 37 %

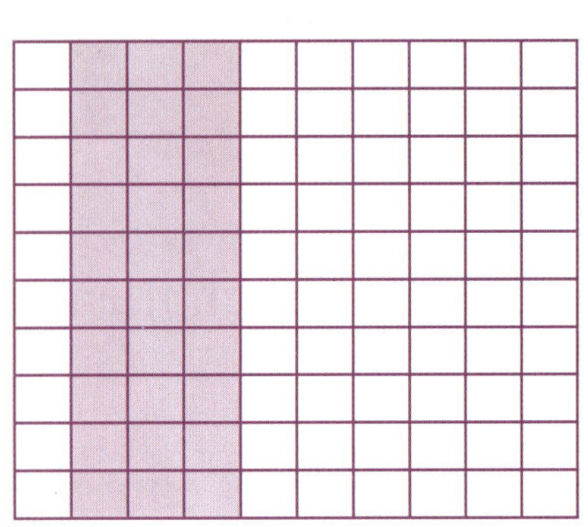

Percentages as Fractions

Let us see what is 20 %?

20 % = 20/100 = (20 ÷ 20) / (100 ÷ 20) = 1/5

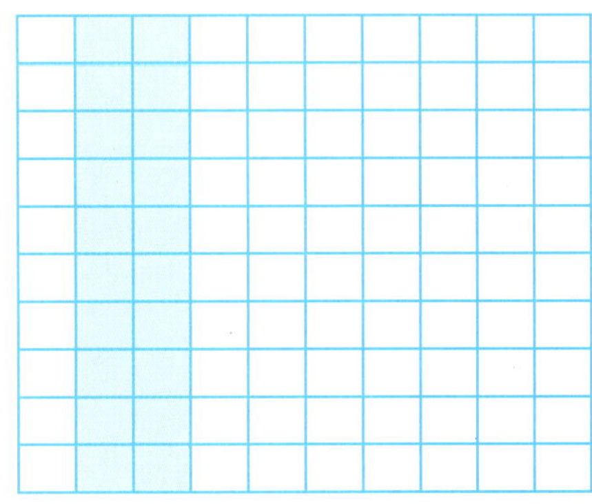

Hence, 20 % = 1/5

EXAMPLE

a. Show 50 % as a fraction

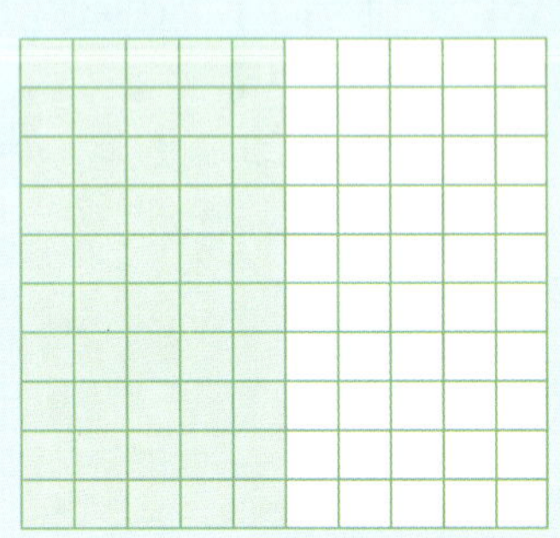

The shaded portion is 50/100 = $\frac{1}{2}$

b. Show 25 % as a fraction

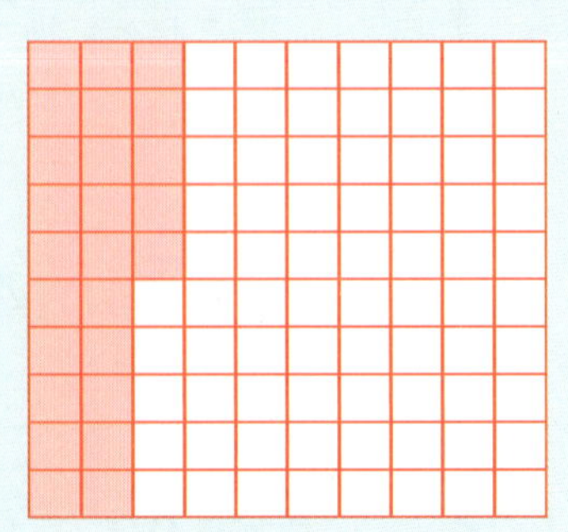

The shaded portion is 25/100 = $\frac{1}{4}$

Percentage into a decimal

38 % = 38/100 = 0.38

120 % = 120/100 = 1.20

9 % = 9/100 = 0.09

Note : To convert percent into fraction place the given number over 100 and reduce to lowest form.

To reduce percentage to decimal write the percent as a fraction with 100 us denominator and write the equivalent decimal.

Exercise 10.1

1. Express the shaded squares in each grid as a fraction,a decimal and percentage.

   21/100 = ______ %

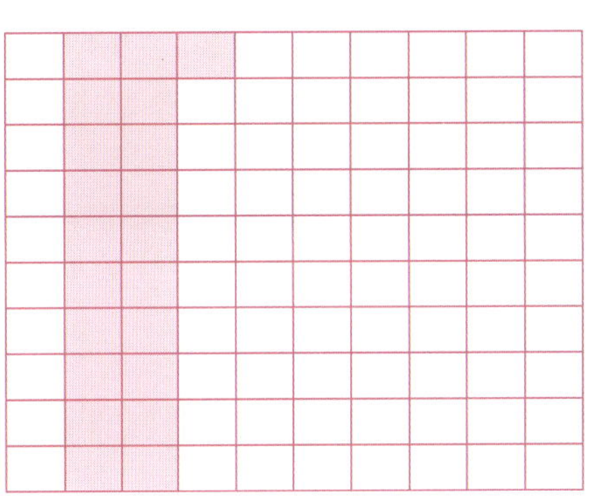

Fractions as Percentages

Grandpa asked Ajay "What is your percentage in the Maths test?"10 year old Ajay thought, "How can I know my percentage as the total marks was only 20.If the test was for 100 marks I could have told Grandpa my percent age". Well ,this is what we all think at that age.But every fraction has an equivalent percentage.

Let us see how?

If we have 18/20 then

Equivalent fraction of 18/20 with denominator 100 is $\frac{18x5}{20x5} = \frac{90}{100}$.

Alternately = (18/20) × 100 %

= 90 %

EXAMPLE

Convert the following fractions into percentage:

(a) 1/5 (b) 3/4

Solution : (a) (1×20) / (5×20) = 20/100 = 20 %

Alternately 1/5 = 1/5 × 100 %

= 20 %

(b) $\frac{3x25}{4x25} = \frac{75}{100} = 75\%$

Alternately $\frac{3}{4} = \frac{3}{4}x100\%$

= 75 %

Decimals as percentages

EXAMPLE

Convert the following decimal numbers into per cent:

(a) 0.7 (b) 0.005 (c) 0.15 (d) 01 (e) 1.93

Solution :

0.7 = 0.7 × 100 % = 70 %

0.005 = 0.005 × 100 % = 5 %

0.15 = 0.15 × 100 % = 15 %

0.1 = 0.1 × 100 % = 10 %

1.93 = 1.93 × 100 % = 193 %

Alternately

$\frac{7x10}{10x10} = \frac{70}{100}$

$\frac{5 \div 10}{1000 \div 10}$ = 0.5/100 = 0.5 %

(15 ÷ 100) = 15 %

(1 × 10) / (10 × 10) = 10/100 =

193/100 = 193 %

Exercise 10.2

1. Write the following as percentages:

   a. 11/25, ¼, 5/7, 1/10 , 7/20 , 14/25 , 21/25 , 13/10 , 28/5 , 42/5, 13/50, 5/12, 1/3

   b. 2.15, 0.28, 0.002, 0.39, 0.75, 0.43, 0.0006, 1.2

2. What percentage of each figure is shaded?

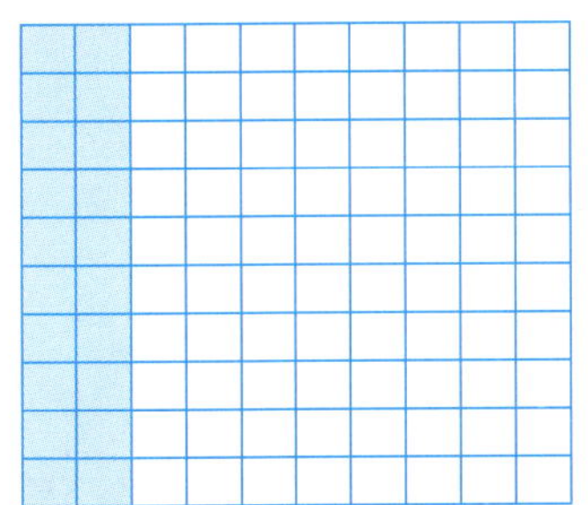
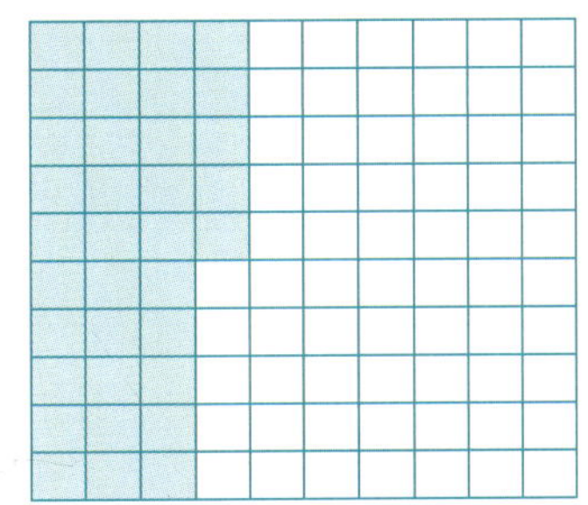
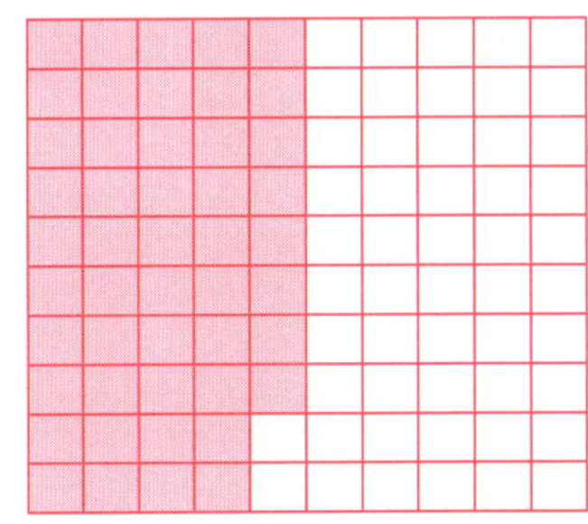

3. Express the percentage as fraction

a. 60 %	b. 12 1/2 %	c. 25 %	d. 16 %
e. 55 %	f. 65 %	g. 75 %	h. 110 %

   (For eg. 60 % = 60/100 = 6/10 = 3/5)

   (For eg. 6 1/4 % = (25/4) 100 = $\frac{25}{4}$x100 =

4. Express the decimal as %

a. 7.3	b. 0.62	c. 0.45	d. 0.05
e. 8.62	f. 13.5	g. 2.42	h. 0.15
i. 0.19	j. 0.01	k. 0.48	

   (For eg. 1.7 % = 1.7 × 100 = 170 %)

5. Express % as decimal :

a. 20 % b. 10.5 % c. 1 % d. 9 % e. 5.5 %

f. 25.2 % g. 14.2 % h. 48 % i. 3 % j. 99 %

(For eg. 45 % = 45/100 = 0.45)

6. Fill in the blanks in the following table:

%	Fraction	Decimal
50	________	0.5
1	1/100	________
________	11/20	0.55
________	________	0.45
75	________	________

Percentage of a number

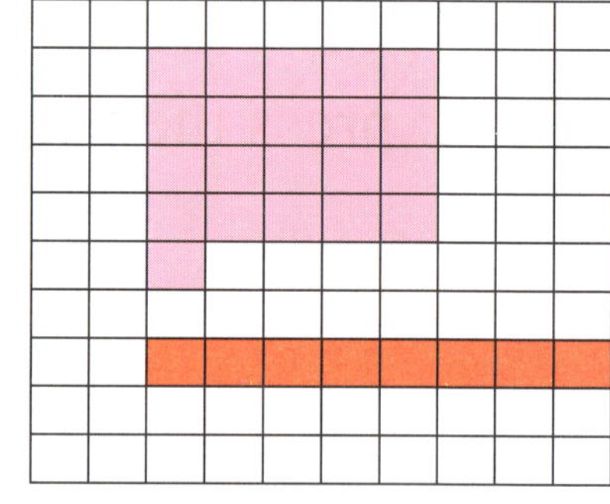

Pink squares are 21 % or 21 out of 100.

And 8 squares in red)

21 % of 100 = 21/100 × 100 = 21

Red squares = 8 out of 100 = 8/100 × 100 = 8

EXAMPLE

Find 40 % of 20

= (40 /100) × 20

= 40/5 = 8

EXAMPLE

Find 55 % of 1500 l

55/100 × 1500 = 55 × 15 = 825 l

Find 75 % of 120 kg

= 75/100 × 120 = ¾ × 120 = 3 × 30 = 90 kg

EXAMPLE

What per cent of 30 is 20?

It is the same as 20 = ______ % of 30 or $\frac{20}{30}$

i.e. 2/3 × 100 % = $66\frac{2}{3}$% of 30 is 20.

Money and Metric Measures as Percentages

You must have often seen in advertisements or banners "10 % off on shirts"or "25 % off on shoes". Well % is often used in connection with money.

- 100 paise = 1 Rupee
  So, 1 paisa = 1/100 of a rupee = 1 % of a rupee
  25 paise = 25 % of a rupee
  83 paise = 83 % of a rupee

- 100 cm = 1 m
  So, 1 cm = 1/100 of a metre = 1 % of a metre
  10 cm = 10 % of a metre, 65cm = 65 % of a metre

- 1000 g = 1 kg
  1 g = 1/1000 = 1/10 × 1/100 = 0.1 /100 = 0.1 % of a kg
  10 g = 10× 0.1 % = 1 % of a kg
  500 g = 0.1 % × 500 = 50 % of a kg

- 1000 ml = 1 l
  So, 1 ml = 1/1000 of a l = 1/10 × 1/100 = 0.1 % of a l
  8 ml = 0.1 % × 8 = 0.8 % of a l
  50 ml = 5 % of a l
  450 ml = 45 % of a l

Exercise 10.3

1. Express the following as percentage of a rupee

   a. 8 paise b. 75 paise c. 50 paise

   d. 19 paise e. 27 paise

2. Express the following as percentage of a metre

   a. 100 cm b. 70 cm c. 3 cm d. 10 cm e. 20 cm

3. Express the following percentage of a kilogram

   a. 1000 g b. 2000 g c. 95 g d. 2 g

   e. 80 g f. 250 g g. 4 kg

Exercise 10.4

1. Colour as directed

   45 % 30 % 8 %

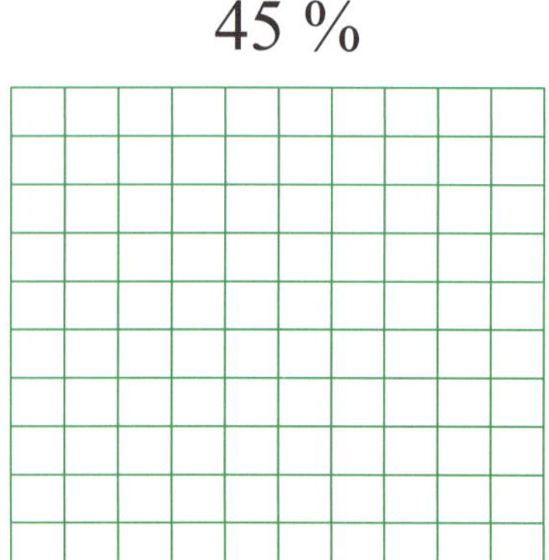

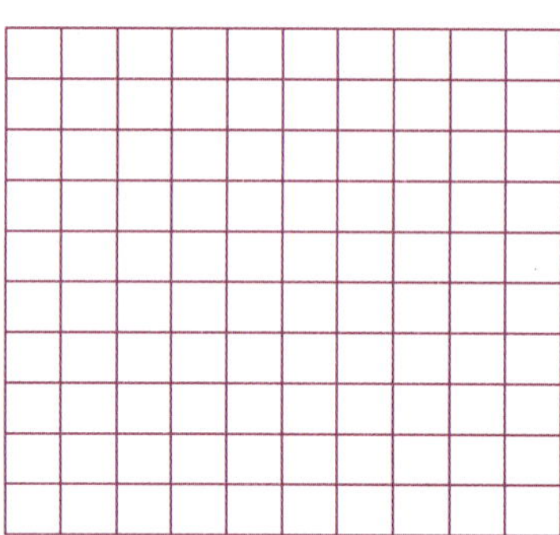

2. Write as a fraction in lowest terms:

   a. 35 % = ________ b. 12 ½ % = ________

   c. 8.25 % = ________ d. 80 % = ________

3. Write as a decimal:

   a. 5 % = ________ b. 15.5 % = ________

   c. 75 % = ________ d. 125 % = ________

4. Fill in the blanks

a. 26/100 = _____%

b. 15 out of 20 = _____%

c. 3/5 = _____%

d. 9/15 = _____%

e. 9/25 = _____%

f. 0.8 = _____%

g. 0.04 = _____%

h. 39/60 = _____%

i. 2 = _____% of 150

j 100 % of 89 = _____

5. Find the value of:

a. 30 % of 50

b. 20 % of ₹ 300

c. 10 % of 80 m

d. 150 % of ₹ 100

e. 0.25 % of 300

f. 3 % of 250 l

g. 14 % of 300 m

h. 4 % of ₹ 80

EXAMPLE

Sally scored 75 % in Science. The test was for 60 marks. What was her score?

Solution: Sally scored 75 % of 60 = 75/100 × 60 = 3/4 × 60 = 3 × 15 = 45.

Hence, Sally scored 45 out of 60 in Science.

Word Problems

1. In an examination, Neha scored 91 % marks out of a total of 600 marks. How many marks did she score?
2. Salman was absent for 28 days out of 210 working days in a year. Find his attendance in percentage for the year.
3. Kareena has ₹ 5000 with her and spends 20 % on a dress. What is the cost of the dress?

4. Earth's surface consists of 75 % water. What fraction is this? Also find the percentage of earth's surface that is land.

5. Abhishek read 48 pages of a 160 page book. What percentage of the book is not read by him?

6. Out of a distance of 1500 km Rohini travelled 75 % by train and the rest by car. Find the distances travelled by train as well as car.

7. Boiled potatoes contains 80 % of water. Express as a fraction.

8. ¾ of an egg's volume is water. Express this as a percent.

9. 60 % of students in a class are girls. If the total number of students in the class are 180, find the number of boys and girls in the class.

10. Indian team won 80 % of the total of 40 matches played. How many matches did this team win?

11. Rahul earns ₹ 75,000 per month and pays 20 % of his salary as rent. What is the monthly rent he pays?

12. The population of a village is 3500 and there are 26 % females. Find the number of females in the village.

13. Manju's weight is 12 % more than Sanju's weight. If Sanju's weight is 60 kg, find Manju's weight.

14. In a classroom 18 students were standing and 32 students were sitting. What percent of students were sitting?

Mental Maths

1. 20 % of 70 __________ 70 % of 20 (Insert > or <)
2. 4 % of 75 = __________.
3. 2 3/8 = __________%
4. 79 % = __________ (fraction).
5. $2\frac{1}{2}$ is __________% of 10.
6. 0.52 = __________%
7. 40 % of __________ is 15.
8. 75 % of 11 kg = __________g.
9. 60 % of $3\frac{1}{4}$ hours = __________ minutes.
10. 27 % of 45 = __________ (in decimals)

11 Data-Handling

Information collected is called **data**. It is presented in different forms like in pictures (pictograph), graphs, pie charts etc.

Data collected is presented in the form of a table or pictures.

EXAMPLE

In the carnival, class V was responsible for the games section. This is how they recorded the data.

Games	Number of people who participated
Ringing the bottle	😊 😊 😊
Throwing the bottle	😊 😊 😊 😊
Throwing the ring	😊 😊 😊 😊 😊
Estimating weight	😊 😊
Dart board	😊 😊 😊

😊 Represents 20 people

This information (data) can be presented in a tabular form also.

Game	Ringing the bottle	Throwing the bottle	Throwing the ring	Estimating weight	Dart board
Number of persons who participated	60	80	100	40	60

From the above table or pictograph we can easily answer questions like.

a. Which game was most popular? Throwing the ring.

b. How many people tried estimating weight? ________

c. What was the average number of people who played a game? ________

d. Which game was least popular? ________

Bar Graph

India is a vast country with a huge population. There are many languages spoken in our country. Let's look at the table.

Language	English	Hindi	Punjabi	Bengali	Tamil
Spoken by (In crores)	70	80	20	35	18

The number of people is very large. It will take a lot of time to draw a pictograph. So, it is better to present the information in the form of a bar graph.

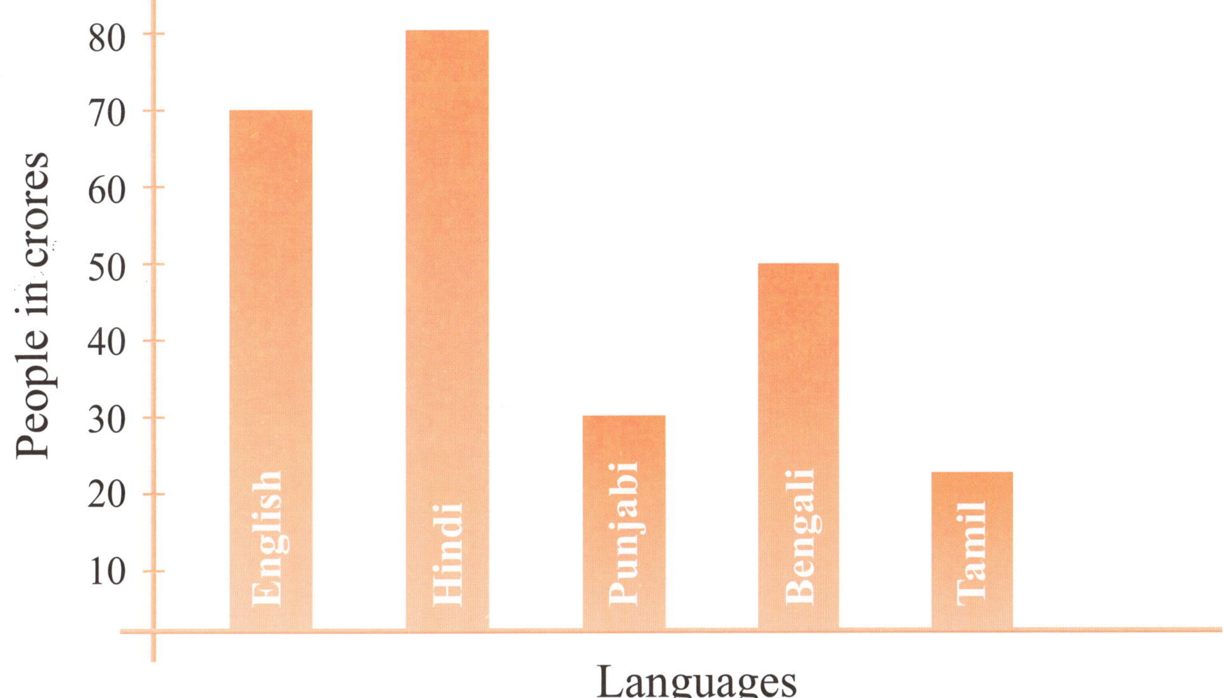

Study the bar graph and answer the following questions.

a. Which is the most commonly spoken language in India? _______

b. About how many people speak Tamil? _______

c. Is Hindi more popular than English? _______

d. How many people speak Bengali and Tamil? (Approx) _______

Exercise 11.1

1. The bar graph shows the preferences of the students in class V for the type of programme they like to watch.

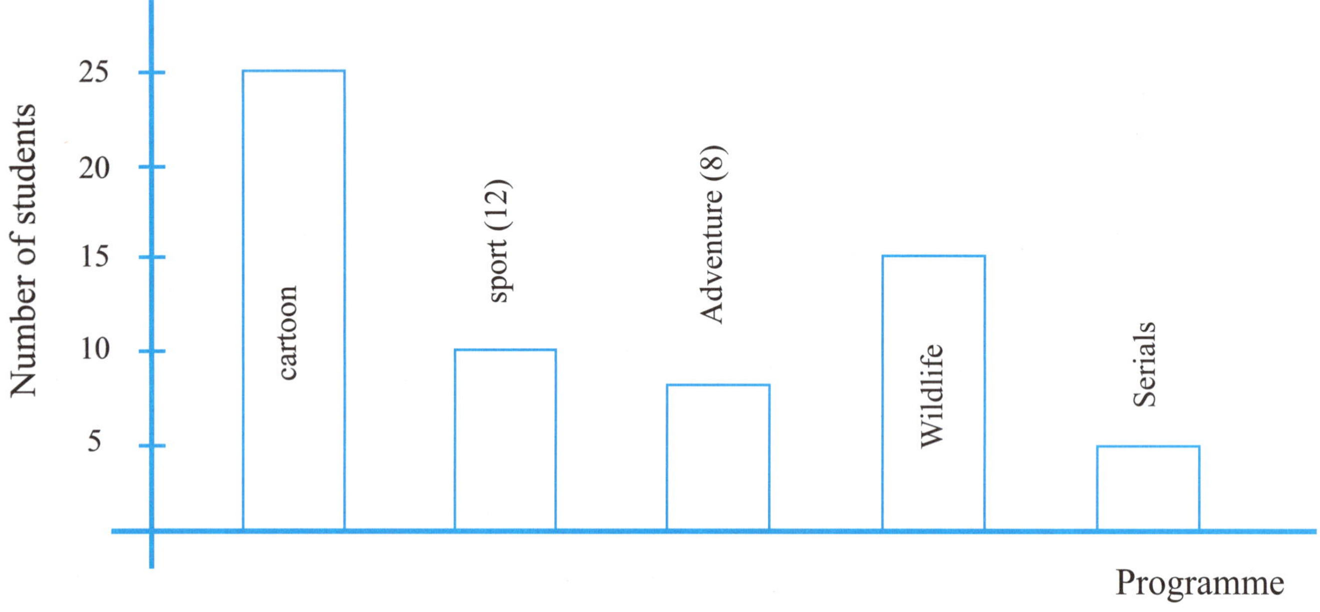

Answer the following questions.

a. Which type of programme is most popular among students of class V?

b. Which programme is least popular?

c. How many children were interviewed?

d. Which is more popular-sports or adventure?

e. What percentage of students like sports?

2. This graph shows the number of students absent in VA during the week (Total strength is 40)

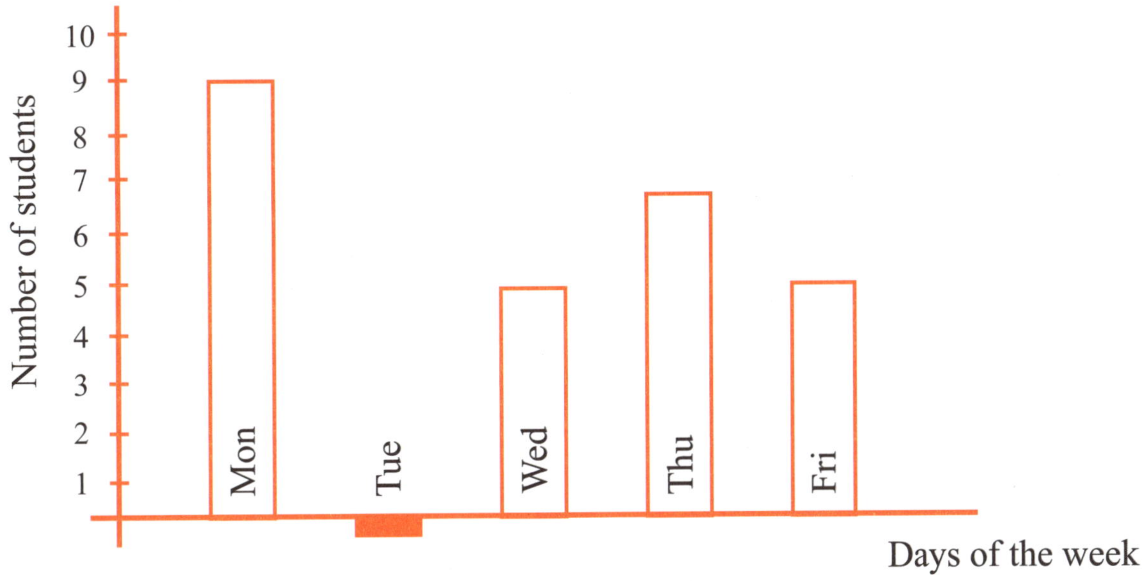

Answer the following questions.

a. On which day were the maximum number of students absent?

b. On which day was the number of absentees the least?

c. Looking at the graph can you guess on which day was a test conducted in this class?

d. What was the total number of absentees?

e. Find the average number of absentees during the week.

3. Mr. Razak has a bakery. He made the following cakes in a day.

Type	Cheese cake	Chocolate	Vanilla	Pineapple
Number	30	40	15	25

Represent the above information pictorially where 1 🧁 represent 10 cakes.

Now answer the following questions.

a. How many cakes did he bake in all?

b. If cost of a chocolate cake is ₹ 20, how much did he get by selling all the chocolate cakes?

c. He sold 95 cakes. How many were left?

d. If he got ₹ 180 by selling the vanilla cakes, find the cost of 1 vanilla cake.

4. Pihu has a collection of toys which is represented like this.

 Represents 2 toys

a. How many dolls does she have?

b. How many balls does she have?

c. What is the total number of toys?

d. What percent of her toys is Teddy bears?

Bills

12

Whenever we buy something from a shop, we get a bill. A bill shows/ reflects the purchases made, their prices and the final amount to be given to the shop. We also get electricity bills, telephone bills, fuel bills etc. These bills tell us how much we have used and how much money is to be paid.

What does a bill contain?

A bill gives us the following information.

a. Name and Address of shop.

b. Bill number

c. Date of Purchase

d. Items purchased

e. Rate or price of each item

f. Quantity or number of each item purchased

g. Total price of each item purchased

h. Total amount to be paid

i. Signature or stamp of the shopkeeper

B. No. 384

A-38, Punjabi Bagh, Delhi

Name. Mr. Rakesh Date 13/10/11

S. No.	Particulars	Qty.	Rate	Cost
1.	Rice	4	45.00	180.00
2.	Soap	6	23.00	138.00
3.	Paste	1	145.00	145.00
4.	Biscuits	2	15.00	30.00
			Total	493.00

Signature

(Verify the bill before paying)

EXAMPLE

Shweta goes to a coffee shop which displays a price list.

Coffee – ₹ 50 Tea – ₹ 35

Burger – ₹ 75 Vegetable sandwich – ₹ 55

Cold coffee with ice cream – ₹ 90

How much would Shweta pay if she ordered 1 coffee, 2 sandwiches, 1 burger and 1 cold coffee with ice cream. Make a bill.

Coffee Shop B. No.

City mall, Chandigarh

Name. Ms. Shewta Date 11/11/11

S. No.	Particulars	Qty.	Rate	Cast
1.	Coffee	1	50	50.00
2.	Sandwiches	2	55	110.00
3.	Burger	1	75	75.00
4.	Cold coffee with ice-cream	1	90	90.00
			Total	325.00

Signature

Shweta pays ₹ 325.00

Exercise 12.1

1. Complete the bills given below as per the rate list.

Fairprice B. No. 84

B-25, Punjabi Bagh, Delhi

Name. Mr. Mehta Date ....

S. No.	Particulars	Rate	Qty.	Cost
1.	Apple	80/kg	2	
2.	Watermelon	30/kg	1	
3.	Potatoes	15/kg	4	
4.	Egg	20/doz	62	
5.	Butter	1/2 kg	120	
		Total		

Apple Store B. No. 85

A- 5/25, Rani Bagh, Delhi

Name. Ms. Kapoor Date ....

S. No.	Particulars	Qty.	Rate	Cost
1.	Mustard oil	4l	85 l	
2.	Sugar	5kg	30/kg	
3.	Jam	2	80/bottle	
4.	Sauce	2	105/bottle	
5.	Cornflakes	1	115/pkt.	
			Total	

2. Make bills for the following purchases.

(Use the price list given below)

a. 4 kg of sugar, 5 kg of potatoes, 3 kg of oil, 1/2 kg butter, cornflakess 2 kg, watermelon 2 kg.

b. 2 kg onions, 1 kg potatoes, 2 dozens of bananas, 2 kg of apples, 1 dozen pencils, 2 tubes of toothpaste, 31 cartons of milk, 3 bulbs

c. 500 g of coffee, 2.5 kg of sugar, 1 kg of tea, 2 bottles of sauce, 2 bottles of jam, 2 bread loaves, 4 cakes of soap.

Price List

Sugar	30/kg	Bulbs	45/bulb
Vegetable oil	90/kg	Milk	50/carton
Butter	120/kg	Potatoes	15/kg
Tea	250/kg	Onions	20/kg
Coffee	300/kg	Apples	80/kg
Bread	20/loaf	Banana	30/doz
Jam	80/bottle	Watermelon	30/kg

Mental Maths

1. Fill in the blanks

   a. 100°C = ______________ °F

   b. 32° F = ______________ °C

   c. 36° F = ______________ 36°C

   d. 212°F = ______________ °C

   e. 90°C = ______________ °F

2. The following graph show the sales of a magazine on different days of a week.

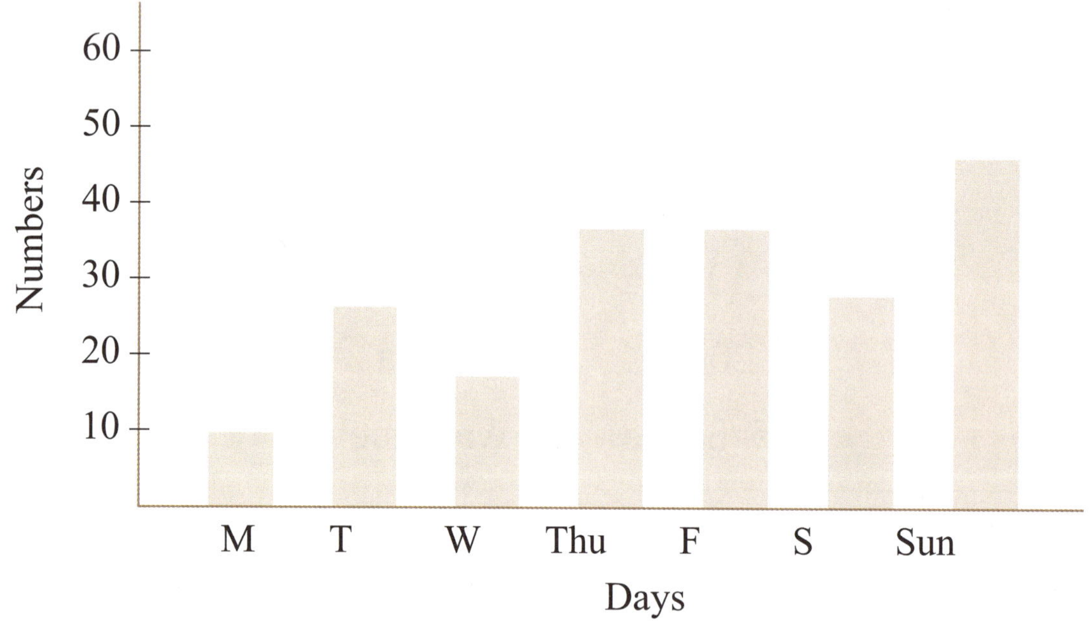

   a. On which day was the sale maximum?

   b. On which 2 days was the sale the same?

   c. On wednesday how many magazines were sold?

   d. Find the average sale per day.

   e. On which day was the sale minimum?

REVIEW EXERCISE 1

1. Fill in the blanks

   a. Twenty three millions seven hundred and nine is ________.

   b. In 36275820, ____ has a value of 5000.

   c. If 4095000 is rounded off to millions place it becomes ________.

2. Using Roman numerals write numerals which is one less than.

   a. LX b. 146 c. M

   d. C e. LXXX f. CL

3. a. Difference of 2 numbers is 196205. If the greater number is 874104, then find the smaller number

   b. Which is greater - successor of 325479 or producessor of 325469.

   c. Find the number that must be subtracted from 2202022 to get 953678?

   d. How many times does the digit 8 occur in tens place in all numbers between 100 and 1000?

4. Write the place value of 5 in each of the following

   a. 150432 b. 126.5

   c. 5,00,000 d. 13.456

5. Fill in the blanks

   a. $700+9+\frac{3}{10}+\frac{6}{1000}=$ ________

b. $11.5 - 2.8 =$ __________

c. $51.789 \times 10 =$ __________

d. $3.403 \times 100 =$ __________

e. _______ $\times 10 = 71$

f. $\frac{7}{8} - \frac{3}{8} =$ __________ or __________

g. $\frac{3}{4} + \frac{7}{12} =$ __________

6. Write the factors of

a. 72 b. 81 c. 64 d. 105

7. Fill in with the prime numbers which are missing

a. ____, ____, 5, 7

b. 19, ____, 29, 31

c. 37, ____, ____, 47

d. 61, 67, ____, 73

REVIEW EXERCISE 2

1. Write in words (Indian and international system) after putting commas accordingly.

   a. 430923 b. 4406007

   c. 504030 d. 600600

2. Write in numerals.

   a. Thirty crores thirty

   b. Seven lakh seven hundred seven

   c. Six lakh sixty

   d. Nine million nineteen

3. The cost of 125 refrigerators is ₹ 2706875. Find the cost of 1 refrigerator.

4. A ship is used to transport containers which weigh 500 kg each. In the ship 24 containers of 500 kg each and 2 containers weighing 300 kg and 325 kg respectively were loaded.

   i. What is the total weight loaded into the ship?

   ii. If the total capacity of the ship is 20000 kg, how much more weight can be loaded into the ship?

5. Sum of 2 numbers is 3148654. If one of the numbers is 1925987. Find the other number.

6. In a car park of a Citysquare hall, there are 38 rows. In each row 113 cars can be parked. What is the maximum capacity of the car park?

7. One kg of potatoes cost ₹ 16. Find the cost of $3\frac{3}{4}$ kg of potatoes

8. What should be added to the difference of 34578 and 29506 to get 100000?

9. A bottle has a capacity of 750 ml. How many litres of juice will be required to fill 13 such bottles?

10. Write in words

    a. 603407 b. 3804009

11. Write in figures

    a. Thirteen lakh seven thousands six

    b. Two lakhs seventeen thousand five hundred and forty.

12. 45.05 m of cloth is needed to make 17 shirts. How much cloth will be needed to make 23 such shirts?

13. Fill in the blanks.

    a. The predecessor of 1 million is _________ (In figures)

    b. Hindu Arabic numeral for LXIX is _________

    c. Rounding 71265 to the nearest ten thousands, is _________

    d. Roman numeral of 89 is _________

    e. Decimal fraction of 0.76 is _________

14. Write in the expanded form

    a. 3598612 b. 589028 c. 4999919

15. Write the successor of

    a. 4000000 b. 39999 c. 999999

16. Write the differences in place values of the two fours in 3405849

REVIEW EXERCISE 3

1. Find the H.C.F. of

   a. 96 and 120 b. 144 and 312 c. 605 and 935

2. Find the LCM of

   a. 115,253 and 69 b. 180,384 and 144 c. 175,182 and 350

3. The HCF of 2 numbers is 15 and their product is 85050. Find the LCM of the 2 numbers.

4. Write all prime numbers from 40 to 60.

5. Find the smallest number divisible by 15, 20 and 27

6. Two ropes 12 m and 18 m long are to be cut into small pieces of equal length. What will be the greatest length of each piece?

7. Use divisibility rule to find which numbers are divisible by 3; by 9

   a. 234567

   b. 99989321

   c. 6910041

8. Express as sum of 2 primes.

   6 = ______ + ______

   8 = ______ + ______

   24 = ______ + ______

   44 = ______ + ______

REVIEW EXERCISE 4

1. Convert the following into improper fraction $2\frac{6}{7}, 3\frac{3}{10}$

2. Convert into mixed fraction $\frac{16}{9}, \frac{31}{6}$

3. Write in lowest form $\frac{115}{207}; \frac{273}{377}; \frac{350}{434}$

4. Find the value of

   a. $1\frac{5}{12}+2\frac{4}{9}+3\frac{1}{6}$

   b. $1-\frac{8}{15}$

   c. $5\frac{2}{3}-2\frac{3}{4}$

   d. $2\frac{1}{3}+3\frac{1}{6}-1\frac{5}{12}$

5. Subtract the su3m of $4\frac{1}{2}$ and $5\frac{3}{8}$ from the sum of $6\frac{3}{4}$ and $7\frac{1}{2}$.

6. A shopkeeper had $47\frac{1}{2}$ m long rope. On Monday he sold $29\frac{1}{3}$ m and on Tuesday. He sold $8\frac{5}{6}$ m. How much rope is left?

7. Express the following as a fraction.

   1. 25 mins as fraction of an hour.
   2. 75 cm as fraction of 1 meter.
   3. 15 hours as fraction of a day.
   4. 65 paise as fraction of a rupee.

8. Multiply

a. $\frac{16}{75} \times \frac{15}{24}$

b. $11\frac{1}{5} \times \frac{17}{28}$

9. Divide

a. $5\frac{1}{3} \div \frac{8}{9}$

b. $21 \div 4\frac{1}{5}$

10. A woman wanted to buy 5 kg of rice from a store. She picked up two $\frac{3}{4}$ kg packets. The rest of the rice she bought in $\frac{1}{2}$ kg packets. How many half kg packets did she buy?

11. Reduce to lowest terms $\frac{119}{153}, \frac{114}{228}, \frac{57}{95}$

12. A drum is $\frac{3}{4}$ full. If 25 l more is required to fill it up, find the capacity of the drum.

13. $\frac{1}{2}, \frac{1}{5}, \frac{1}{3}, \frac{1}{10}$ write the smallest fractions, the biggest fraction.

14. Write in descending order.

a. $\frac{4}{9}, \frac{8}{3}, \frac{5}{6}$

b. $\frac{3}{8}, \frac{1}{4}, \frac{5}{7}$

15. Write equivalent fraction of

a. $\frac{18}{24} = \frac{144}{\square}$

b. $\frac{70}{85} = \frac{14}{\square}$

d. $\frac{3}{4} = \frac{\square}{48}$ e. $\frac{66}{242} = \frac{3}{\square}$

16. Fill in the blanks

a. $2\frac{1}{3} - 1\frac{2}{3} = \square$ b. $7\frac{2}{5} - \square = 3\frac{1}{5}$

c. $\frac{16}{5} - \square = \frac{7}{5}$ d. $\frac{12}{15} - \square = \frac{7}{15}$

17. Convert to decimals

$\frac{3}{5}, \frac{1}{125}, \frac{1}{20}, \frac{3}{250}$

18. If $69 \times 19 = 1311$ then find.

a. $6.9 \times 19 =$ ____________

b. $6.9 \times 1.9 =$ ____________

c. $0.69 \times 1.9 =$ ____________

d. $0.69 \times 190 =$ ____________

e. $0.69 \times 0.019 =$ ____________

REVIEW EXERCISE 5

1. What percentage of 12 is 9?
2. What percentage of 1 hour 20 min is 24 minutes?
3. Evaluate

   a. $\frac{1}{2}$ of $10+9-(9+7)\div4-3x2$

   b. $\frac{2}{3}x\frac{1}{4}+\frac{3}{4}\div\frac{9}{28}$

4. Find the volume of a cube whose side measures 4 cm.
5. Determine area of a square field of perimeter 80 m.
6. The weekly income of 4 brothers is ₹ 1330.25, ₹ 1350.30, ₹ 1430.25 and ₹ 1450.50. Find their average income.
7. Find the cost of carpeting a room which is 6 m long and 4.5 m broad, at the rate of ₹ 55 per square meter.
8. How much time will elapse from 3.05 pm to 5.23 pm?
9. Find the area of a field 6 m long and 4.5 m wide.
10. A car travels 436.8 km in 7 hours. Find the distance covered in 1 hour.
11. Samara reached a mall at 6.50 pm. and left after 3 hours 25 minutes. At what time did she leave the mall?
12. The Super Market has installed scanners for checking out the customers. The average time for a check out of a customer is $2\frac{1}{2}$

minutes. How many customers on an average, can they check out in half an hour?

13. Human body consists of $\frac{2}{3}$ water.

    a. What percentage is this?

    b. How much water will be there in a person weighing 90 kg?

14. Mehul's marks were:

    a. English: $\frac{18}{20}$ b. Maths: $\frac{24}{25}$ c. French: $\frac{15}{15}$

    Change them into percentage.

15. A brick measures 20 cm × 10 cm × 35 cm. How many bricks will be required to make a wall of dimensions 25 m × 2 m × 3.5 m?

16. Find the volume of milk in a container of dimensions 11 × 8 × 10 cm?

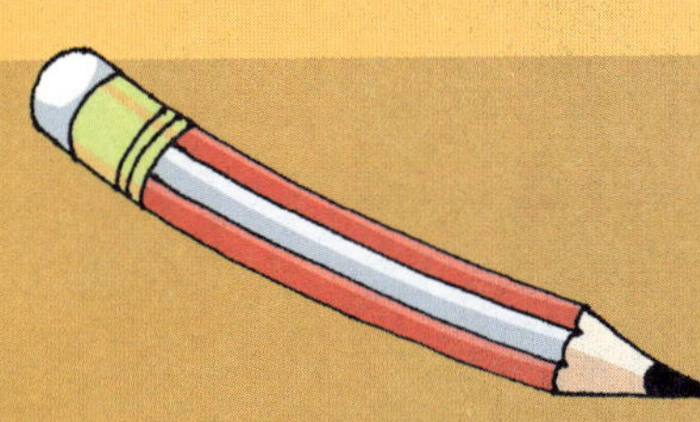

Activity

	÷	4	=	4		10	×		=	500		100
×		×				×		÷				÷
6	×		÷	5	=	24		10	×	10	=	
=		÷		×		×		=		=		×
	÷	8	=	12			÷	5	=	50		25
		=		÷		=						=
100	×	10	×		=	60,000		75	÷		=	25
				=						×		
	÷	18	=	1		864				21		
×		÷			49		7	×	2	=	14	
3	×	9	=	27		4				63		2
=		=		+		=						×
54	×		+	108	=	216		108	÷	9	=	
				=								=
810	÷	6	=			12	×		÷	4	=	24

Answers

Revision

1. a. Thirty four thousand one hundred seventeen.
   b. Two lakh seventeen thousand one hundred forty eight.
   c. Five hundred seventy five thousand four hundred thirty nine.
   d. Six hundred thousand three hundred six.
   e. Nineteen lakhs thirty
   f. Eight hundred fifty thousand thirteen

2. a. 20,004 b. 50,016 c. 9,00,010 d. 6,05,060 e. 70,070

3. a. 100 b. 1000 c. 1000

4. 72,200

5. a. 10,369 b. 8,75420

6. 1009999 7. 47123 8. 173787

9. a. 264320 b. 764000 c. 255000 d. 67900 e. 41,20,000

10. a. 420783 b. 172975 c. 4791000 d. 453871 e. 1386639

11. a. 14114.98 b. 709.04 c. 716.26 d. 103.67 e. 1001

12. a. 48 b. 59

Exercise 2.1

1. a. 6,00,000 b. 20,000 c. 6,00,00,000 d. 10,00,000 e. 80,00,000
   f. 60,0,00,000

4. a. 3,20,00,00, b. 69,00,70,019 c. 40,00,00,014
   d. 50,05,25,500 e. 13,20,05,000

Exercise 2.2

1. a. 80000000 + 8000000 + 100 + 30

   b. 70000000 + 1000000 + 100000 + 30000 + 4000 + 10 + 1

c. 10000000 + 6000000 + 500000 + 30000 + 8000 + 400 + 20 + 7

d. 4000000 + 600000 + 40000 + 400 + 40

2. a. 10000010 b. 6,74,58,021 c. 5932781 d. 70007070

3. a < b. < c. > d. < e. < f. < g. > h. >

4. a. 13936025; 13930625; 13903625; 13093625

b. 5476321; 5476312; 5476132; 5471632

c. 39765234; 39672534; 37965234; 36795234

d. 4671390; 3457619; 3456719; 1234567

5. a. 8787878; 8787887; 8787888; 8787897

b. 21977861; 2225861; 2308651; 2328561

c. 18634695; 22700329; 43214598; 90478110

d. 44488141; 44688141; 46488114; 46488141

6. a. 99,99,999 b. 10,00,00,000 c. 9,99,99,999 d. 10000001

e. successor

7. a. 103469; 964310 b. 1045789; 9,99,99,999

c. 60789; 98760 d. 1025689; 9865210

Exercise 2.3

1. a. 600,435,070 b. 945,367,008 c. 200,012,001

d. 22,222,222, e. 702,702,702 f. 60,001,003

2. a. 80,000 b. 800,000

c. 3,000,000 d. 70,000

e. 600,000 f. 3,000

g. 0 h. 100,000,000

3. a. 70,030,090 b. 88,000,200 c. 3,003,003

d. 440,404,044 e. 00,065,236

4. 2. hundred thousand 3. 10 crores 4. 10 mill

5. a. = b. < c. < d. >

6. Lucknow – 21,85,927 Hyderabad – 36,37,483

Pune – 25,38,476 Bangaluru – 43,01,326

Chennai – 43,43,645 Kolkata – 95,72,876

Delhi – 98,79,172 Mumbai – 1,19,78,450

Exercise 2.4

1. a. 20,112,204 b. 9,473807 c. 473,838

 d. 6,849,056 e. 43,590,828 f. 28,443,694

2. a. 1,644,423 b. 41,75,400 c. 3,012,494 d. 2,00,47,096 e. 24 corores

3. a. 93,448 b. 5,782,319 c. 5341301 d. 7,4651,165 e. 100,001

4. a.

	8 0 7 0 4 2 5 3
+	9 4 5 2 3 4 6
+	4 6 7 2 8 5 2
	9 4 8 2 9 4 5 1

b.

	2 0 6 3 0 1
+	3 4 9 2 5
+	6 9 5 6 7 0
	9 3 6 8 9 6

c.

	2 6 5 7 9 6
+	1 5 4 6 3 7
	4 2 0 4 3 3

d.

	9 2 7 4 7 7 5
−	6 9 4 4 7 3 3
	2 3 3 0 0 4 2

e.

	6 2 0 4 0 2
−	2 9 5 6 7 0
	3 2 4 7 3 2

f.

	4 0 0 0 0 0 0 0
−	2 6 4 6 2 5 1 4
	1 3 5 3 7 4 8 6

Exercise 2.5

1. a. 6,75,012 b. 2390273
   c. 6521625 d. 4118814
   e. 8532652 f. 10742680
   g. 71874014 h. 5189745
   i. 3908304 j. 7245200
2. a. 9788750 b. 3542500kg c. 1259250kg
   d. 467250 e. 1,681,200 f. 291,600

Exercise 2.6

1. a. Q = 727, R = 11 b. Q = 418, R = 140 c. Q = 2586, R = 142
   d. Q = 941, R = 541 e. Q = 98, R = 261 f. Q = 12, R = 2236
   g. Q = 974, R = 56 h. Q = 4810, R = 305
2. a. 90 bags b. 730 c. 34 guns
   d. 8624 boxes e. Q = 367, R = 264 f. 9998856

Exercise 2.7

1. a. XLVI b. LIII c. LXXXV
   d. LXV e. LXIX f. XCLL
2. a. 54 b. 95 c. 59
   d. 45 e. 94 f. 49
   g. 99 h. 92

Exercise 2.8

1. a. MDL b. MDCCCLXXXV c. MCDLXXXLL
   d. MMX e. MMDCCLX f. CCXCV
2. a. 1905 b. 1670 c. 2219
   d. 747
3. a. – b. MCMXLVLL c. MCMXIX
   d. MCMLXIX e. MCMIII

Mental Maths

1. 1107
2. 999999
3. 10000001
4. 21,930,419
5. 999999
6. 396
7. 102345
8. 987654
9. 10
10. 610600

Exercise 3.1

1. a. 2×2×3×3 b. 2×2×2×7 c. 2×2×2×2×2×2
   d. 3×5×5 e. 2×2×5×5 f. 2×2×2×2×7
   g. 2×2×2×3×5 h. 2×2×2×2×2×5

2. a. 72

   2 36

   2 18

   2 9

   3 3

   b. 128

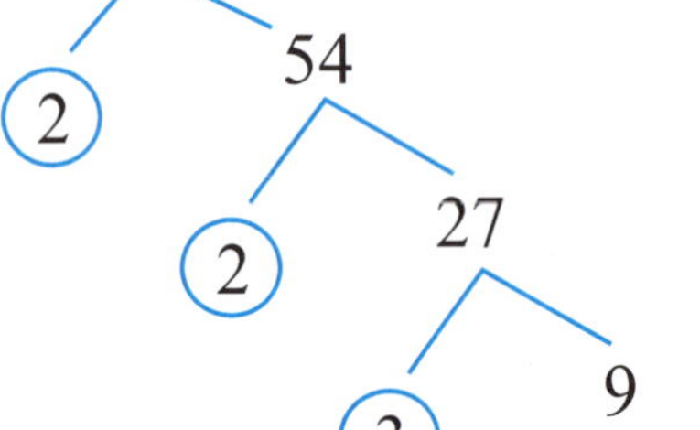

   c. 48

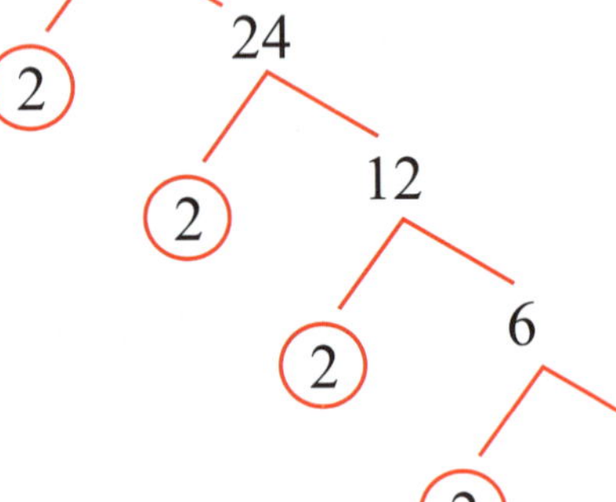

   d. 42

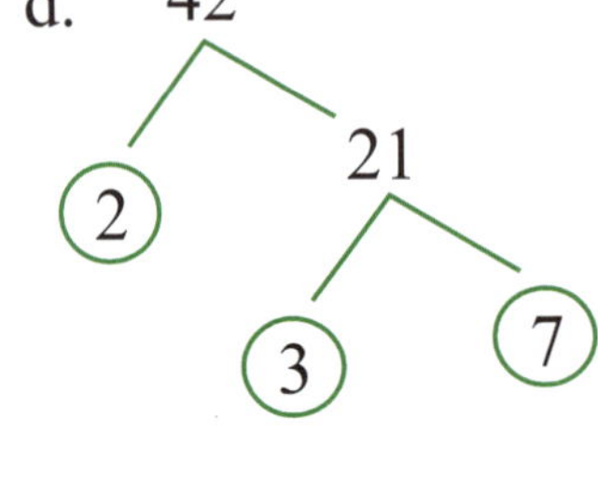

3. Between 2 and 80
   21 and 40
   41 and 60
   61 and 80
   81 and 100

4. 1 to 40 – 2, 4, 6, 8, 9, 10, 12, 14, 15, 16, 18, 20, 21, 22, 24, 25, 26, 27, 28, 30, 32, 33, 34, 35, 36, 38, 39

91 to 100 – 92, 94, 95, 96, 98, 99

41 to 90 – 42, 44, 45, 46, 48, 49, 50, 51, 52, 54, 55, 56, 57, 58, 60, 62, 63, 64, 65, 66, 68, 69, 70, 72, 74, 75, 76, 77, 78, 80, 81, 82, 84, 85, 86, 87, 88

Exercise 3.2

1. a. 6 b. 54 c. 44 d. 14
   e. 21 f. 24 g. 28 h. 2

2. a. 1 b. 14 c. 90 d. 272
   e. 38 f. 12 g. 30 h. 38

Exercise 3.3

1. a. 1020 b. 32 c. 54 d. 54
   e. 84 f. 72

2. a. 150 b. 1008 c. 1728 d. 1050

Exercise 3.4

1.

Numbers	Product	HCF	LCM
8, 30	240	2	120
32, 36	1152	4	288
	612	9	68

2. a. 36, 28
   36 = 2 × 2 × 3 × 3
   28 = 2 × 2 × 7
   LCM = 252

   b. 78

3. 48 4. 126 5. 330

Exercise 3.5

Number	2	3	4	5	6	9	10
84	✓	✓	✓	×	✓	×	×
919	×	×	×	×	×	×	×
2340	✓	×	✓	✓	×	×	✓
5475	×	✓	×	✓	×	×	×
66660	✓	✓		✓	✓	×	✓

Exercise 4.1

1. a. $\frac{2}{4} = \frac{1}{2}$ b. $\frac{4}{5}$ c. $\frac{7}{9}$

2. a. 4/9 b. 2/11 c. 2/5

Exercise 4.2

1. a. $\frac{2}{7}$ c. $\frac{5}{8}$ d. $\frac{15}{18}$ g. $\frac{17}{19}$ h. $\frac{10}{11}$

2. b. $\frac{9}{5}$ e. $\frac{14}{11}$ g. $\frac{19}{3}$ h. $\frac{14}{13}$

Exercise 4.3

1. a. 1 b. 4 c. 24 d. 7
   e. 82 f. $2\frac{2}{5}$ g. $\frac{59}{20}$ h. $7\frac{1}{3}$

2. a. $2\frac{3}{4}$ b. $2\frac{6}{7}$ c. $10\frac{1}{3}$ d. $3\frac{1}{7}$
   e. $3\frac{1}{8}$ f. $1\frac{4}{9}$ g. $2\frac{4}{5}$ h. $3\frac{1}{6}$

3. a. $\frac{31}{6}$ b. $\frac{13}{2}$ c. $\frac{25}{7}$ d. $\frac{49}{12}$

e. $\frac{26}{11}$ f. $\frac{57}{10}$ g. $\frac{16}{13}$ h. $\frac{29}{4}$

Exercise 4.4

1. a. $\frac{2}{9}$ b. $\frac{4}{13}$ c. $\frac{1}{8}$ d. $\frac{7}{5}$

2. a. $\frac{5}{6}$ b. $\frac{7}{10}$ c. $\frac{1}{3}$ d. $\frac{8}{15}$

3. a. $\frac{1, 4, 8, 9}{11}$ b. $\frac{10, 11, 12, 13, 26}{25}$

4. a. $\frac{2}{5}, \frac{2}{7}, \frac{2}{8}, \frac{2}{11}$ b. $\frac{10}{11}, \frac{10}{17}, \frac{10}{19}, \frac{10}{21}$

Exercise 4.5

1. a. $\frac{13}{15}$ b. $\frac{17}{12}$ c. $\frac{7}{9}$ d. $\frac{11}{10}$

e. $\frac{11}{8}$ f. $\frac{11}{12}$ g. $\frac{6}{4}$ h. $\frac{29}{24}$

i. $\frac{71}{40}$ j. $\frac{43}{30}$ k. $\frac{17}{8}$ l. $\frac{13}{12}$

2. a. $\frac{31}{12} = 2\frac{7}{12}$ b. $11\frac{7}{9}$ c. $11\frac{7}{9}$ d. $6\frac{3}{4}$

e. $11\frac{11}{72}$ f. $5\frac{5}{6}$ g. $9\frac{5}{21}$ h. $8\frac{5}{24}$

i. $7\frac{3}{10}$ j. $6\frac{13}{20}$ k. $7\frac{26}{45}$ l. $6\frac{11}{42}$

Exercise 4.6

1. a. $\frac{1}{2}$ b. $\frac{3}{4}$ c. $\frac{12}{13}$ d. $\frac{5}{6}$

   e. $\frac{5}{7}$ f. $\frac{1}{6}$ g. $\frac{4}{7}$ h. $\frac{4}{9}$

2. a. $\frac{4}{12}=\frac{1}{3}$ b. $\frac{1}{8}$ c. 0 d. $\frac{13}{24}$

   e. $\frac{1}{4}$ f. $\frac{1}{2}$ g. $\frac{1}{20}$ h. $\frac{9}{70}$

   i. $\frac{7}{33}$ j. $\frac{1}{16}$ k. $\frac{1}{12}$ l. $\frac{4}{63}$

3. a. $1\frac{5}{6}$ b. $1\frac{5}{18}$ c. $1\frac{3}{5}$ d. $5\frac{1}{2}$

   e. $1\frac{17}{24}$ f. $2\frac{1}{8}$ g. $2\frac{17}{63}$ h. $1\frac{17}{20}$

   i. $2\frac{1}{4}$ j. $\frac{1}{4}$ k. $1\frac{1}{2}$ l. $2\frac{3}{4}$

Exercise 4.7

1. $6\frac{3}{4}$ 2. $54\frac{1}{8}$ 3. $2\frac{1}{10}$ 4. $2\frac{23}{60}$ 5. $2\frac{1}{3}$

Exercise 4.8

1. a. 5 b. $\frac{28}{5}$ c. 6 d. 18 e. 0

   f. $\frac{9}{19}$ g. $\frac{2}{3}$ h. 8 i. $\frac{5}{3}$ j. $\frac{9}{4}$

2. a. $\frac{16}{21}$ b. $\frac{2}{15}$ c. $\frac{5}{12}$ d. $\frac{77}{16}$ e. $\frac{4}{5}$

f. $\frac{1}{7}$ g. $\frac{7}{32}$ h. $\frac{2}{9}$ i. $\frac{1}{3}$ j. $\frac{7}{12}$

k. $\frac{1}{5}$ l. $\frac{1}{8}$ m. $\frac{1}{16}$ n. $\frac{1}{6}$ o. $\frac{3}{8}$

p. $\frac{3}{2}$ q. 15 r. $\frac{3}{10}$ s. $\frac{1}{6}$ t. $\frac{2}{21}$

3. a. $\frac{12}{7} = 1\frac{5}{7}$ b. $1\frac{1}{5}$ c. 2 d. $3\frac{2}{5}$ e. 24

f. $\frac{7}{3} = 2\frac{1}{3}$ g. 9 h. 2

Exercise 4.9

1. a. $\frac{4}{8}$ b. $\frac{13}{10}$ c. $\frac{9}{1}$ d. $\frac{7}{13}$ e. $\frac{7}{19}$

f. $\frac{14}{51}$ g. $\frac{9}{41}$ h. 1

2. a. 18 b. $\frac{13}{2}$ c. 27 d. 24 e. 30

f. 9 g. 40 h. 9 i. 22 j. $\frac{1}{5}$

3. a. $\frac{6}{7}$ b. 51 c. 15 d. 1 e. $\frac{5}{3}$

f. 6 g. 13 h. $\frac{3}{2}$ i. $\frac{2}{3}$ j. ??

Exercise 4.10

1. 15 cups 2. 80 3. 25 4. 14 5. $2\frac{1}{7}$

6. 60,000 7. $\frac{1}{4}$ 8. 15 9. 24 10. ₹ 1800

Mental Maths

1. a. F b. F c. F d. T e. F

2. a. $\frac{1}{3600}$ b. 140L c. $\frac{8}{10}$ d. one-third e. 48

Exercise 5.1

1. a. $10+3+\frac{2}{10}+\frac{7}{100}$ b. $40+8+\frac{5}{10}+\frac{8}{100}+\frac{6}{1000}$ c. $300+10+4+\frac{6}{10}$ d. $60+9+\frac{3}{1000}$

   e. $9+\frac{4}{100}$ f. $700+30+5+\frac{2}{10}+\frac{6}{100}+\frac{4}{1000}$ g. $4+\frac{9}{10}+\frac{8}{100}$ h. $10+\frac{1}{1000}$

2. a. 20.68 b. 300.406 c. 4.084 d. 30.039 e. 42.503

   f. 11.111 g. 24.41 h. 0.055 i. 0.022

Exercise 5.2

1. a. b b. 3.8 c. 1.45 d. 0.27

2. a. $\frac{6}{100}$ b. 30 c. $8+\frac{1}{100}$ d. $7+\frac{2}{10}+\frac{9}{100}$ e. 2.36

   f. 6.258 g. 4.061 h. 0.304 i. 0.111 j. 6.02

Exercise 5.3

1. a. 0.29 b. 0.6

2. a. < b. > c. > d. > e. <

   f. < g. > h. > i. < j. <

3. a. 5.014 < 5.14 < 5.14 < 6.041 b. 3.07 < 3.17 < 3.78 < 3.87

   c. 5.09 < 5.38 < 5.83 < 6.9 d. 9.05 < 9.35 < 19.03 < 19.51

4. a. 70.21 > 70.063 > 7.63 > 7.6 b. 10.8 > 10.05 > 10.048 > 10.023

   c. 5.3 > 5.03 > 4.6 > 4.58 d. 49.4 > 49.35 > 4.96 > 4.935

5. a. 7.7; 7.8; 7.9 b. 1.19; 1.20; 1.21
c. 9.007; 9.008; 9.009 d. 17.89; 17.90; 17.9

Exercise 5.4

1. a. 36.66 b. 26.246 c. 558.65 d. 27.08 e. 31.34
f. 20.701 g. 105.56 h. 8.148

2. a. 0.758 b. 0.517 c. 4403.7

Exercise 5.5

1. a. 1.23 b. 0.549 c. 0.9 d. 20.803 e. 5.821
f. 6.08 g. 1.18 h. 54.81 i. 0.362 j. 39.51

2. a. 3.985 b. 12.91 c. 8.318 d. 1.078 e. 1.42
f. 7.22 g. 23.547 h. 18.604 i. 0.903 j. 0.027

Exercise 5.6

1. a. 1.08 b. 0.24 c. 0.12 d. 2.07 e. 7.2
f. 3.64 g. 7.36 h. 201.02 i. 3.36 j. 5.53
k. 906.28 l. 511.11 m. 856.68 n. 325.39 o. 194.4
p. 0.148 q. 2155.5 r. 77.91 s. 112.06 t. 21.2

2. b. 56 hundredth = .56 c. 138 thousand the = .138
d. 126 tenths = 12.6 e. 184 hundredths = 1.84
f. 56 thousand ths = .056

3. a. ₹ 1500 b. 86 litres

Exercise 5.7

1. a. 500.8 b. 2306 c. 98 d. 61100.5 e. .5
f. 7710 g. 11001 h. 40.2 i. 1572 j. 1600
k. 2609 l. 30 m. 790 n. 90.8 o. 4004.1

2. a. 7.155 b. 145.332 c. 30.5214 d. 132.12 e. 1.5
f. 4.263 g. 4.2014 h. 253.8789 i. 261.25 j. 0.084
k. 63.7105 l. 0.03375 m. 653.2 n. 0.028 o. 1.044

3. 1. 34.8 2. 7. 3. .09 4. 0.0087 5. 0.0003
6. 0.1625 7. 8.532 8. 0.027

4. a. 41.6646 b. 4.16646 c. 4.16646 d. .0416646

Word Problems

a. ₹ 378 b. 316.4 c. 164 kg

Exercise 5.8

1. a. 2.4 b. 1.6 c. 1.25 d. 8.1 e. 10.1
f. 13.1 g. 0.61 h. 7.1 i. 0.21 j. 7.63
k. 6.1 l. 4.1 m. 0.05 n. 0.08 o. 0.09

Exercise 5.9

1. a. 5.9 b. 0.04 c. 0.053 d. 0.24 e. 0.051
f. 1.28 g. 0.4 h. 0.31 i. 3.15 j. .28
k. 1.54 l. 0.07 m. 1.4058 n. 8.475 o. 12.65
p. 7 q. 15.24 r. 16.97 s. 3.155 t. 10.4
u. 13.475

Exercise 5.10

1. a. 24.32 b. 0.283 c. 0.0675 d. 0.02 e. 0.0236
f. 0.01 g. 0.07565 h. 0.006 i. 1.264 j. 0.01927
k. 0.028 l. 0.0738 m. 4.29 n. 0.16 o. .265

2. a. 19.157 b. 0.0621 c. 0.76 d. 0.1631 e. 0.01232
f. 0.0941 g. 0.0134 h. 0.515 i. 0.733

3. a. 10 b. 1000 c. 100 d. 10000 e. 1000
f. 10 h. 100 g. 10

Exercise 5.11

1. a. 510 b. 61 c. 31 d. 61.2525 e. 74.7
   f. 77 g. 310 h. 3.7 i. 1524 j. 30
   k. 20 l. 78

Exercise 5.12

1. a. 0.75 b. 0.125 c. 0.625 d. 0.25 e. 0.6
   f. 0.1 g. 2.2 h. 7.5 i. 5.778 j. 5.167
   k. 6.25 l. 0.583

2. 6.23 3. 105 4. 0.75 m 5. 1.758 kg 6. 17
7. 0.023 8. 1.03 kg

Exercise 5.13

1. a. 7 b. 12 c. 8 d. 21
   e. 142 f. 1 g. 0 h. 20

2. a. 65 b. 5.8 c. 11 d. 130.8
   e. 16.3 f. 227.2 g. 28.4 h. 44.4

3. a. 7.33 b. 0.28 c. 1.33 d. 10
   e. 0.67 f. 4.01 g. 0.06 h. 0.04

4. a. 0.13 b. 1.33 c. 0.18 d. 0.47

Mental Maths

1. a. 0.017 b. 6.6 c. 200.02 d. 909.009 e. 2046.708

2. a. < b. like c. = d. $50+0+\frac{3}{10}+\frac{7}{100}+\frac{9}{100}$
   e. 40, 40

Exercise 6.1

1. a. 26 b. 21 c. 1 d. 10 e. 2/15
   f. 6.5 g. 7.08 h. 39 i. 0.95 j. 22/63
   k. 17/4 l. 3/2

2. a. 41 b. 68 c. 12 d. 8 e. 13.125
   f. 84 g. 1/21 h. 6/17 i. 1 j. 94.4

3. a. 4.27 b. 245/36 c. 3 d. 23
e. 39 f. 40

Exercise 7.2

1. ii, iv, v, vi
2. ∠MNT, ∠ABC, ∠POQ, ∠SR, ∠XYZ
3. i. ∠AOB, ∠OBOC, ∠AOC ii. ∠YXZ, ∠WXZ, ∠YXW
   iii. ∠ACO ∠AOD, ∠BOC, ∠AOB, ∠COD
   iv. ∠RTS, ∠RTY, ∠YTX, ∠XTP, ∠PTQ, ∠QTS, ∠STR; ∠STV, ∠RTX, ∠XTQ, ∠QTR

Exercise 7.7

1. Radius – 3.5, 2.4, 4.2
   Diameter – 5, 5.25, 7.2, 1.2
2. centre O
   diameter AB
   3 radii OA, OB, OX
   2 chords XY, AB,

Mental Maths

1. a. F b. F c. F d. F e. T
2. a. centre b. semi-circle c. 7 d. 180° e. Line segment

Exercise 8.1

1. 1. 12 cm_2 b. 9 q cm c. 10 sq cm d. 18 sq cm e. 12 sq cm
   6. 5 sq cm
2. 5 sq cm 12 sq cm 4 sq cm 3 sq cm 16 sq cm
3. a. 6 sq cm b. 10 sq cm c. 26 sq cm d. 10 sq cm

Exercise 8.2

1. 1. 3.5 sq cm 2. 12 sq cm 3. 3 sq cm 4. 10 sq cm 5. 17 sq cm
   6. 5 sq cm

Word Problems

1. 15.75 sq cm 2. 51 sq cm 3. ₹ 150,000 4. 6

Exercise 8.3

1. a. 36 cm^3 b. 64 cm^3 c. 56 cm^3 d. 80 cm^3
2. a. 75 cm^3 b. 91.125 cm^3 c. 1000 cm^3 d. 1953.125 cm^3
   e. 19.683 cm^3
3. a. 120 cm^3 b. 81 cm^3 c. 157.5 cm^3 d. 10.488 cm^3
4. 900 cm^3 5. 1.44 m^3

Mental Maths

2. a. 9 sq cm b. 50 sq cm

Exercise 9.1

1. 88.75 2. 6.2 3. a. 30.5 b. 3.3 c. 85
4. 5.5 5. 39.6 6. a. 37 b. 2 c. 3

Exercise 9.2

1. ₹ 60 2. 2850 kg 3. 6 hours 4. 385 km
5. ₹ 9100 6. 16488 bulbs

Exercise 9.3

1. a. 68 °F b. 86 °F c. 32 °F d. 176 °F e. 104 °F f. 212 °F
2. a. 30 °C b. 45 °C c. 90 °C d. 70 °C e. 35 °C f. 60 °C
3. 37.8 °C 4. 50 °F

Mental Maths

1. a. 0.5505 b. 4 c. 5.6 d. 10 35/36 e. 73.5

   a. B b. C

Exercise 10.2

1. a. 44, 25, 71.4, 10, 35, 56, 84, 130, 560, 840, 26, 41.7, 33.3
   b. 216 %, 28, 0.2 %, 39 % 75, 43, 0.06 %, 120 %

3. a. 3/5 b. 1/8 c. 1/4 d. 4/25 e. 11/20 f. 13/20
   g. 3/4 h. 11/10

4. a. 730 % b. 62 c. 45 d. 5 e. 862 % f. 1350
   g. 242 h. 15 i. 19 % j. 1 k. 48

5. a. 20 b. 0.105 c. 0.01 d. 0.09 e. 00055 f. 0.252
   g. 0.142 h. .48 i. 0.03 j. .99

6.

%	Fraction	Decimal
50	1/100	0.5
1	1/100	0.01
55	11/20	0.55
45	9/20	0.45
75	3/4	0.75

Exercise 10.3

1. a. .08 % b. .75 c. .5 d. .19 e. .27

2. a. 100 % b. 70 % c. 30 % d. 10 % e. 20 %

3. a. 100 % b. 200 % c. 9.5 % d. 0.2 % e. 8 %
   f. 25 % g 400 %

Exercise 10.4

2. a. 7/20 b. 1/8 c. 33/400 d. 4/5

3. a. 0.5 b. .155 c. .75 d. 1.25

4. a. 26 b. 75 % c. 60 d. 60 e. 36 f. 80
g. 4 h. 65 i. 4/3 j. 89

5. a. 15 b. ₹ 60 c. 8m d. ₹ 150 e. .75 f. 7.51
g. 42m h. ₹ 3.20

Word Problems

1. 546 2. 13 1/3 % 3. ₹ 1000 4. 3/4 5. 70 %
6. 1125 km 7. 4/5 8. 75 % 9. 72; 108 10. 32
11. 15,000 12. 910 13. 67.2 kg 14. 64 %

Mental Maths

1. = 2. 3 3. 237.5 4. 79/100 5. 25
6. 52 7. 37.5 8. ??? 9. 117 10. 12.15

Exercise 11.1

1. a. Cartoon b. Serials c. 65 d. Sports e. 18.46%

2. a. Mon b. Tue c. Tue d. 26 e. 5.2

3. a. 110 b. ₹ 800 c. 15 d. 12

4. a. 8 b. 7 c. 23 d. 17.39%

Mental Maths

1. a. 212 b. 0 c. < d. 100 e. 194
2. a. Sun b. Thu, Fri c. 20 d. 31.7 e. Mon

Review Exercise 1

1. a. 23,000,709 b. 5 c. 4,000,000

2. a. LIX b. CXLV c. CMXCIX d. XCIM e. LXXIX
f. CXLIX

3. a. 677899 b. 325479 c. 1248344 d. 90

4. a. 50,000 b. 5/10 c. 500000 d. 5/100

5. a. 709.306 b. 8.7 c. 517.89 d. 3403 e. 71
   f. 4/3 or 1/2 g. 16/12
6. a. 36, 72 b. 1, 3, 9, 81 c. 1, 2, 4, 8, 64 d. 1, 5, 3, 7, 21, 105, 35
7. a. 2, 3 b. 23 c. 41, 43 d. 71

Review Exercise 2

1. a. Four lakh thirty thousand nine hundred twenty three
   b. Forty four lakh six thousand and seven
   c. Five lakh four thousand thirty
   d. Six lakh six hundred
2. a. 30,00,00,030 b. 7,00,707 c. 6,00,060 e. 9,000,019
3. 21,655 4. (i) 12,625 kg (ii) 7375 kg
5. 1222667 6. 4294 7. Rs 60
8. 94928 9. 9750 ml
10. a. Six lakh three thousnad four hundred and seven
    b. Thirty eight lakhs four thousand and nine
11. a. 13,07,006 b. 2,17,540
12. 60.95m
13. a. 99,999 b. 69 c. Seventy thousand d. LXXXIX
    d. 76/100
15. a. 4000001 b. 40,000 c. 10,00,000 16. 399960

Review Exercise 3

1. a. 24 b. 24 c. 55
2. a. 759 b. 5760 c. 31850
3. 5670 4. 41, 43, 47, 53, 57, 59 5. 2700 6. 6 m
7. a. by 3 b. no c. by 3
8. 3, 3 3, 5 11, 13 7, 37

Review Exercise 4

1. $\frac{20}{7}, \frac{33}{10}$

2. $1\frac{7}{9}; 5\frac{1}{6}$

3. $\frac{3}{9}; \frac{21}{29}; \frac{25}{31}$

4. a. $6\frac{31}{36}$ b. $\frac{7}{15}$ c. $2\frac{11}{12}$ d. $4\frac{1}{12}$

5. $4\frac{3}{8}$

6. $9\frac{1}{3}$ m

7. a. $\frac{5}{12}$ b. $\frac{3}{4}$ c. $\frac{5}{8}$ d. $\frac{13}{20}$

8. a. $\frac{2}{15}$ b. 18

9. a. 6 b. 5

10. 7

11. $\frac{7}{9}, \frac{1}{2}, \frac{3}{5}$

12. 1001

13. $\frac{1}{10}; \frac{1}{2}$

14. a. $\frac{8}{3}, \frac{5}{6}, \frac{4}{9}$ b. $\frac{5}{7}, \frac{3}{8}, \frac{1}{4}$

15. a. $\frac{18}{24} = \frac{144}{192}$ b. $\frac{70}{85} = \frac{14}{17}$ c. $\frac{3}{4} = \frac{36}{48}$ d. $\frac{66}{242} = \frac{3}{11}$

16 . a. $\frac{2}{3}$ b. $4\frac{1}{5}$ c. $\frac{9}{5}$ d. $\frac{4}{15}$

Review Exercise 5

1. 0.6, 0.008, 0.05, 0.012

2. a. 131.1 b. 13.11 c. 1.311 d. 131.1 e. .01311

Review Exercise 6

1. 75%
2. 13.11
3. a. 4 b. 10/3
4. 64 cm^3
5. 400 m^2
6. 1390.33
7. ₹ 1485
8. 2 hr 18 mins
9. 27 m^2
10. 62. 4 km
11. 10.15
12. 12
13. a. 66.7% b. 60 kg

14. a. 90% b. 96% c. 100%

15. 25000 16. 880 cm^2

Activity

16	÷	4	=	4		10	×	50	=	500		100
×		×				×		÷				÷
6	×	20	÷	5	=	24		10	×	10	=	100
=		÷		×		×		=		=		×
96	÷	8	=	12		250	÷	5	=	50		25
		=		÷		=						=
100	×	10	×	60	=	60,000		75	÷	3	=	25
				=						×		
18	÷	18	=	1		864				21		
×		÷			49	÷	7	×	2	=	14	
3	×	9	=	27		4				63		2
=		=		+		=						×
54	×	2	+	108	=	216		108	÷	9	=	12
				=								=
810	÷	6	=	135		12	×	8	÷	4	=	24